Mandala
Technical Coloring Books

Copyright: Published in the United States by Fred Sanchez
Published December 2016
ISBN-13: 978-1541255340
ISBN-10: 1541255348

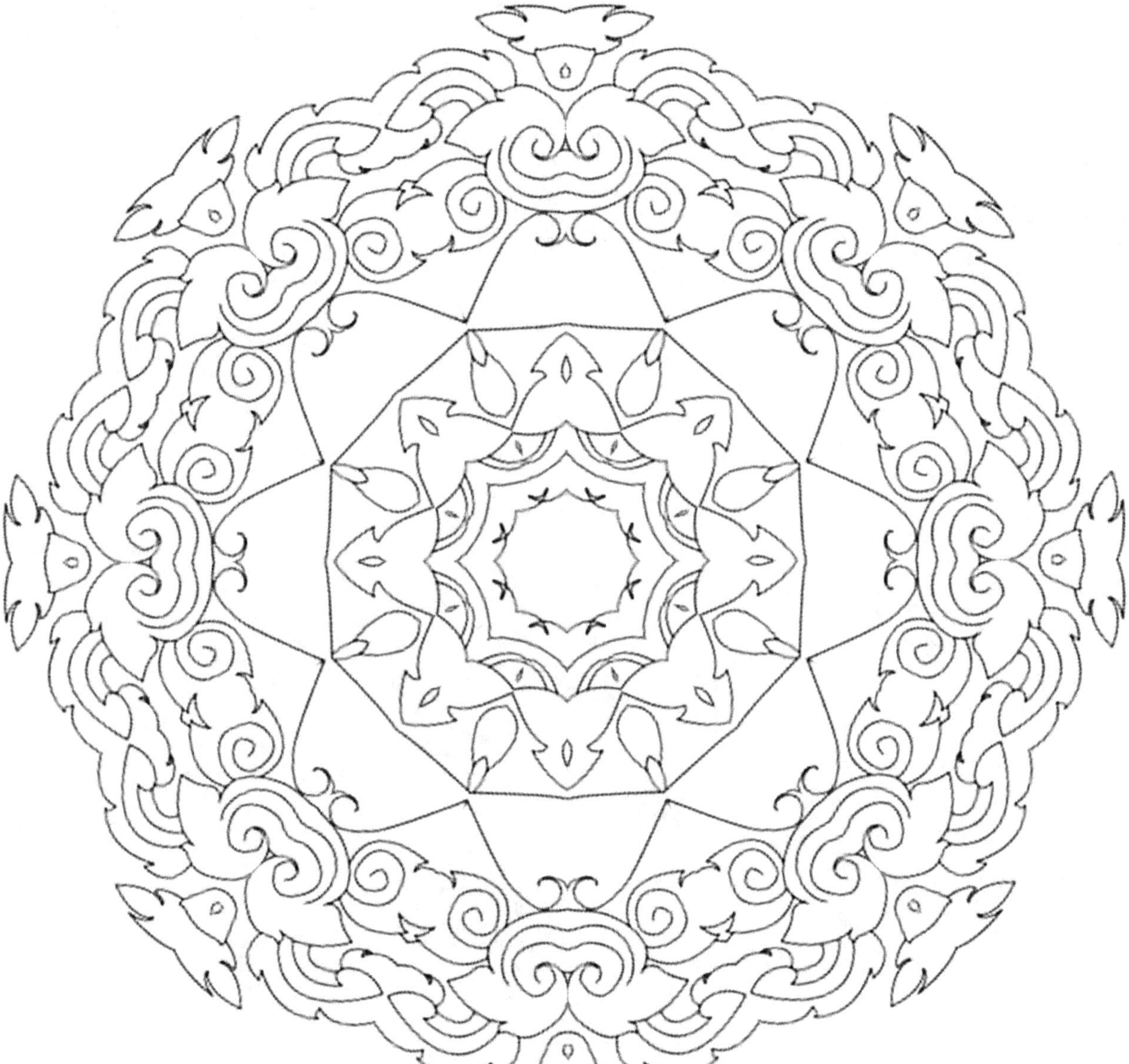

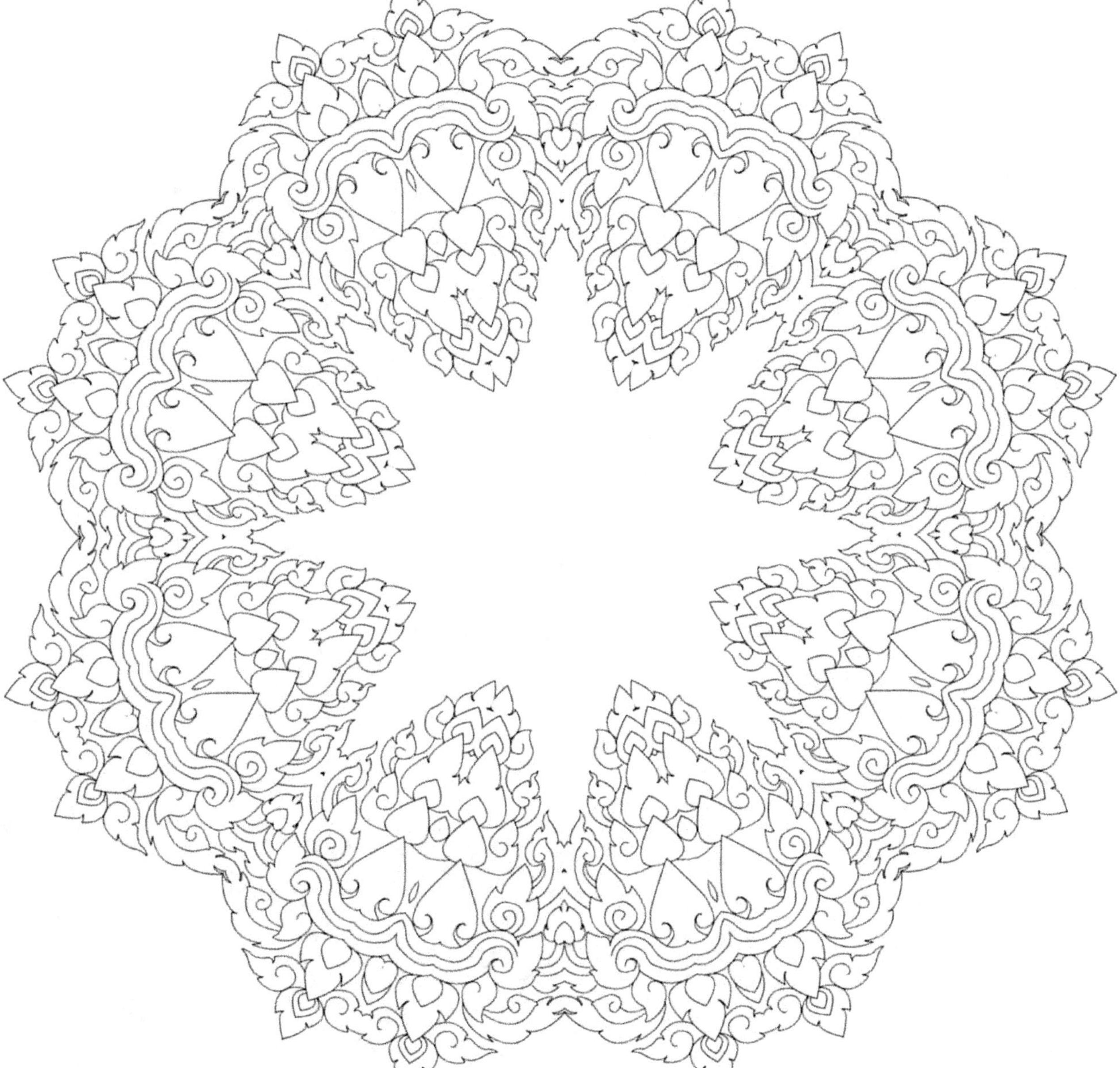

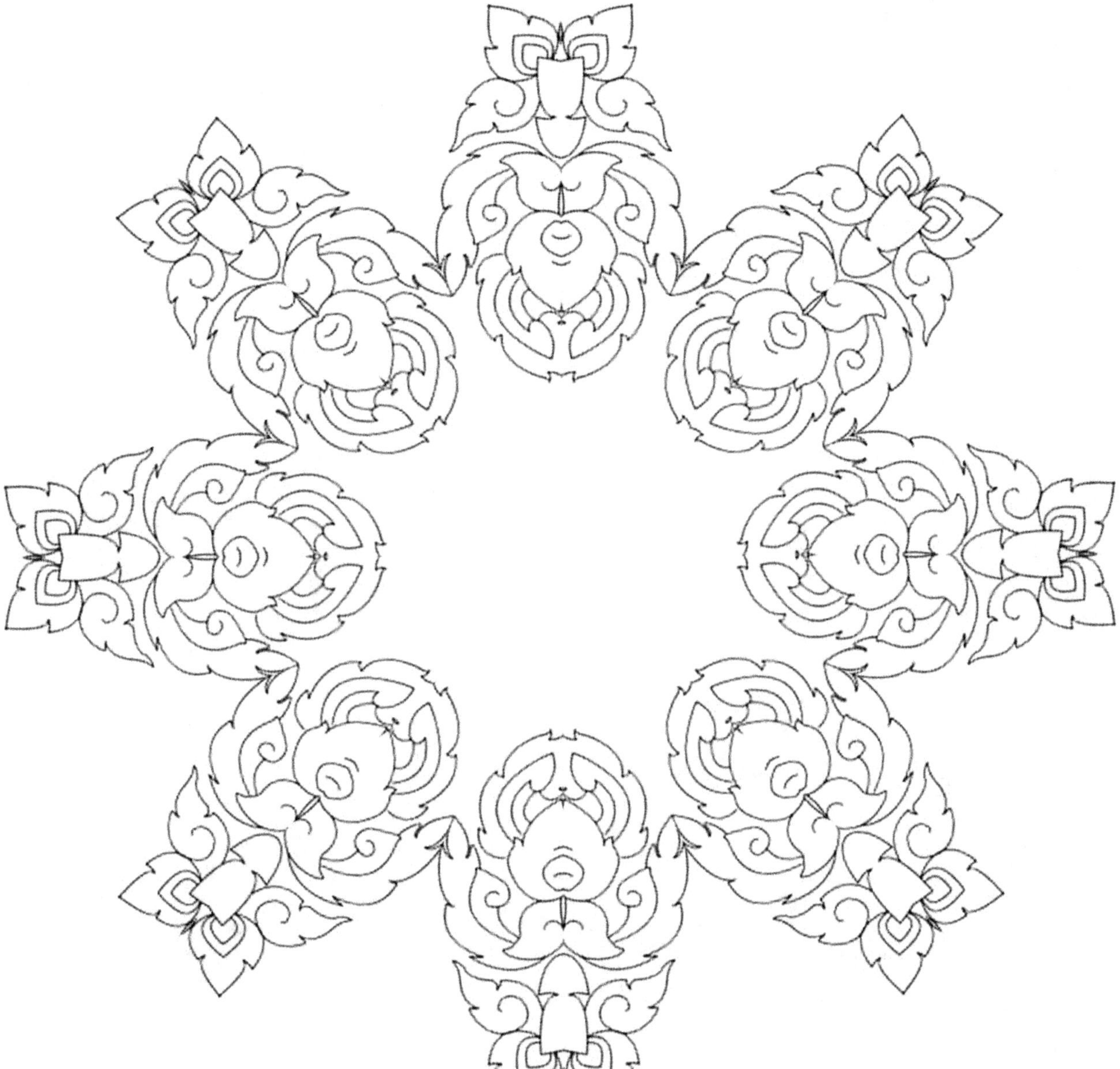

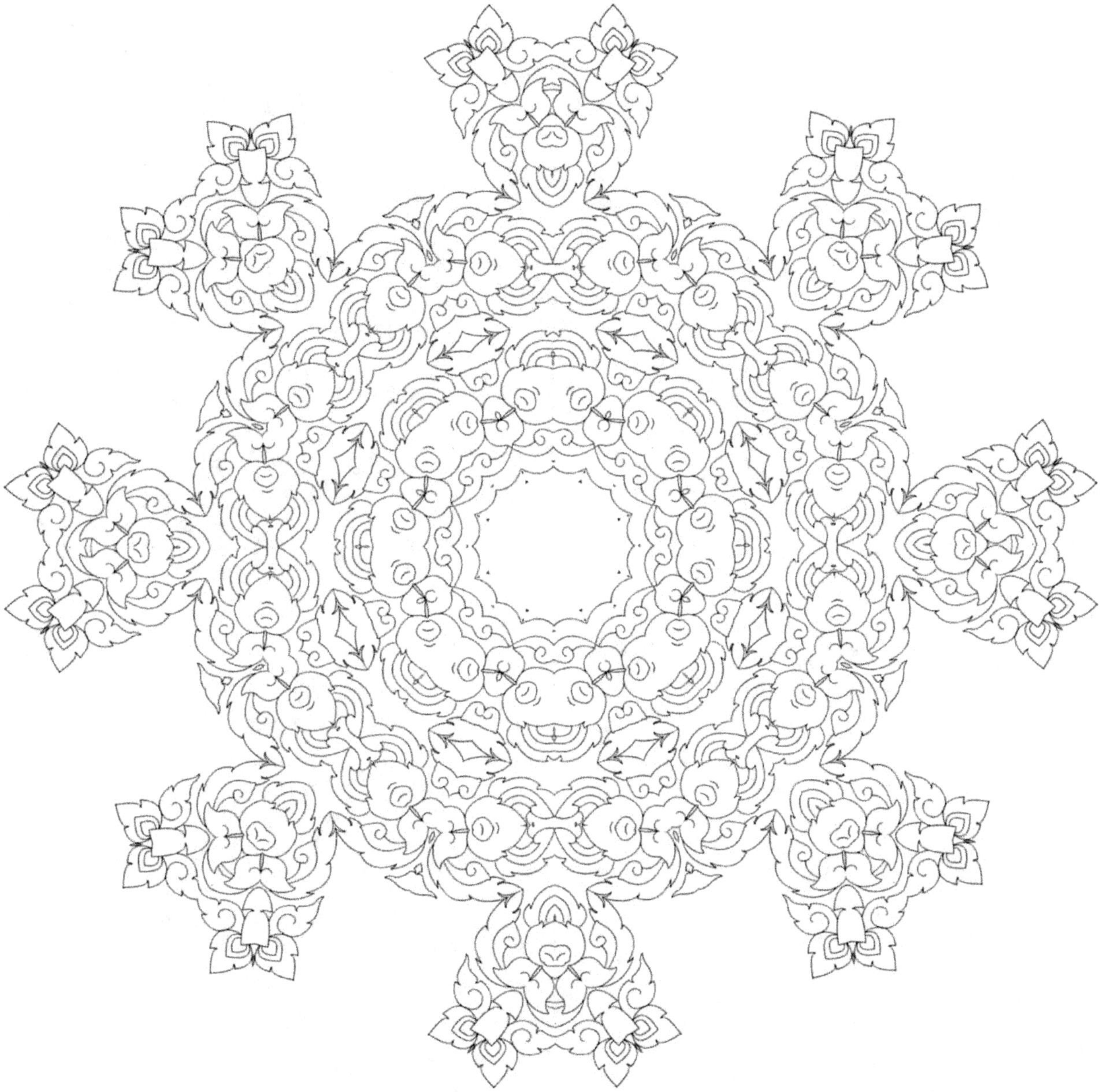

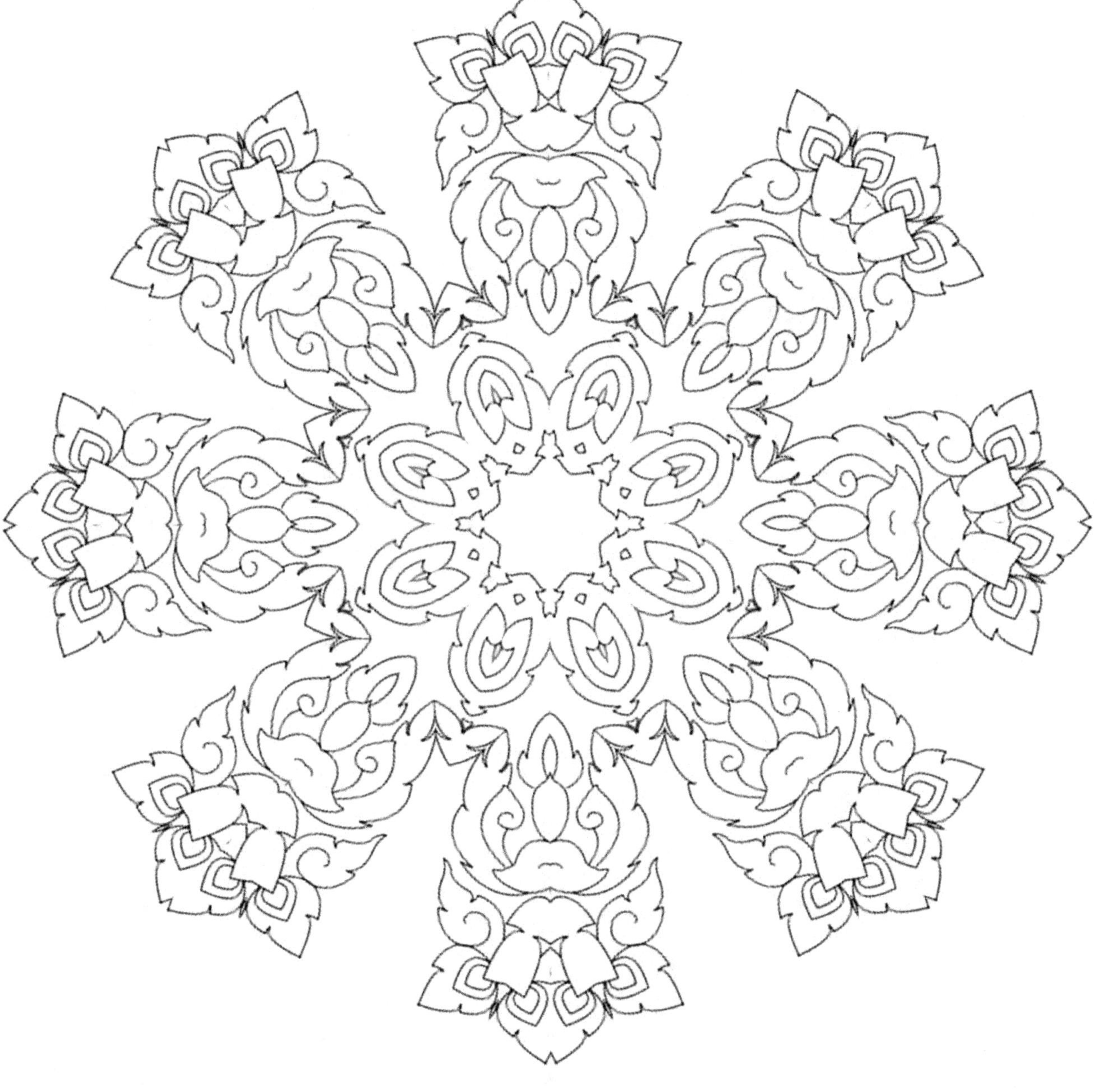

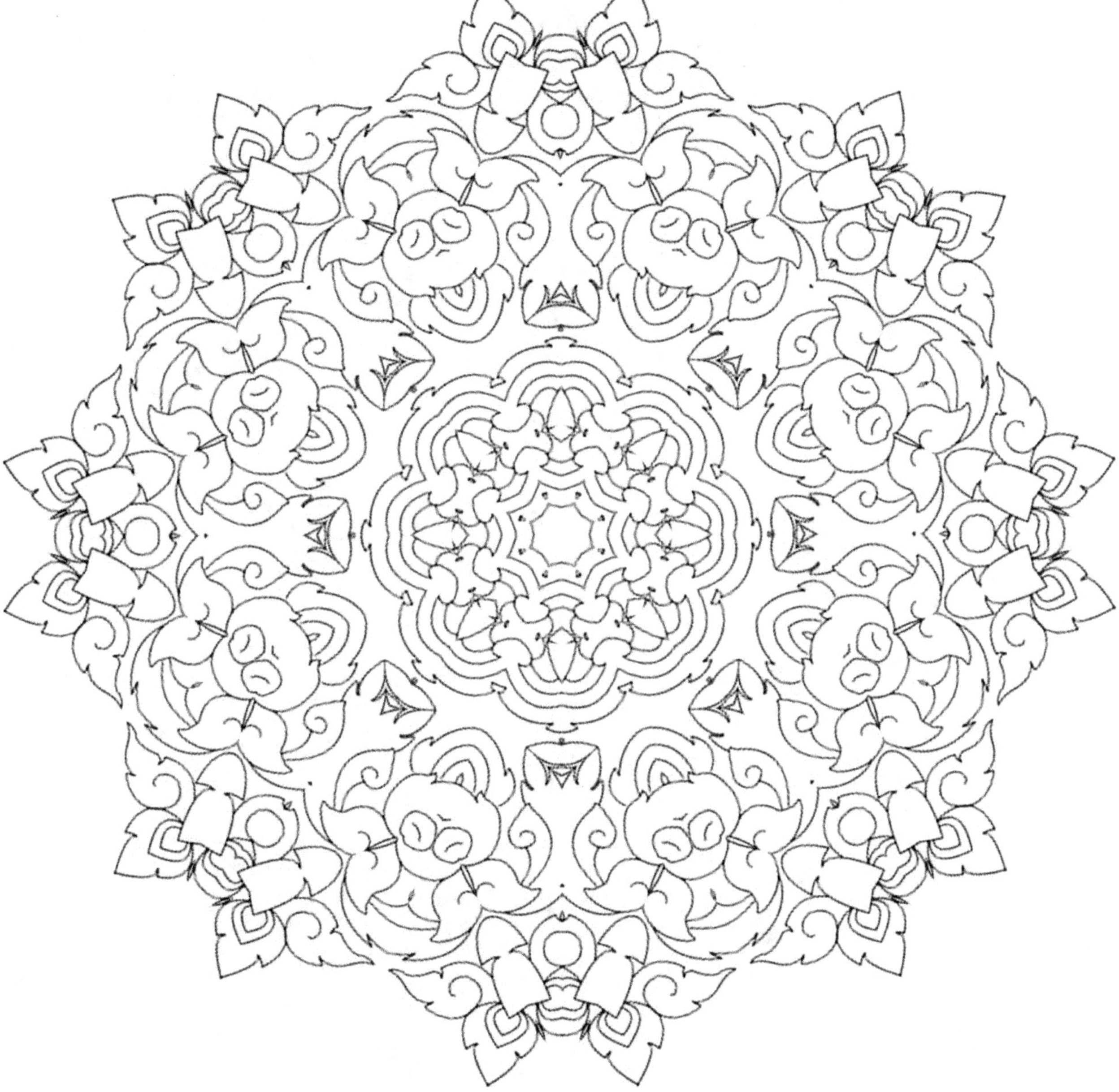

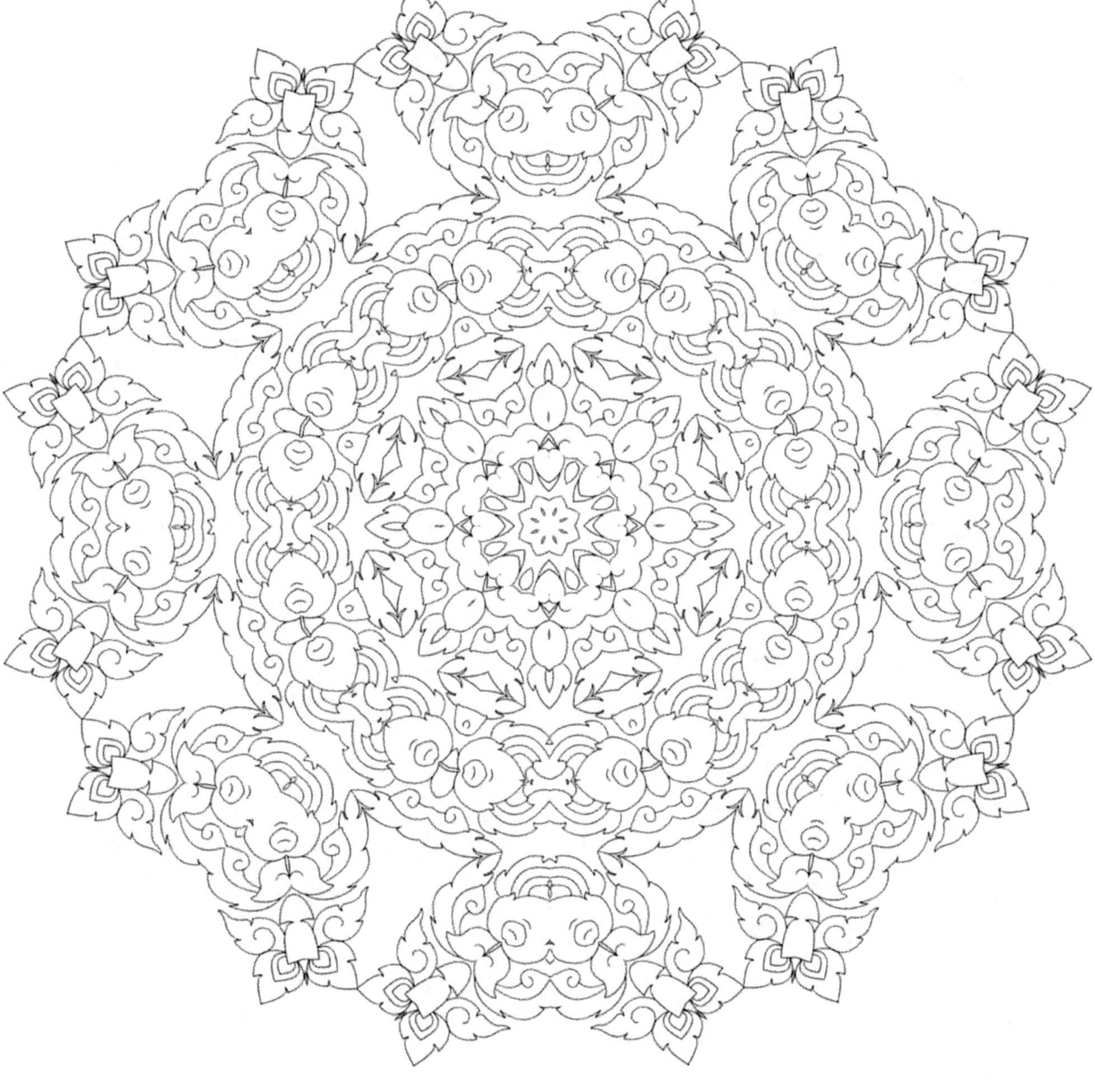

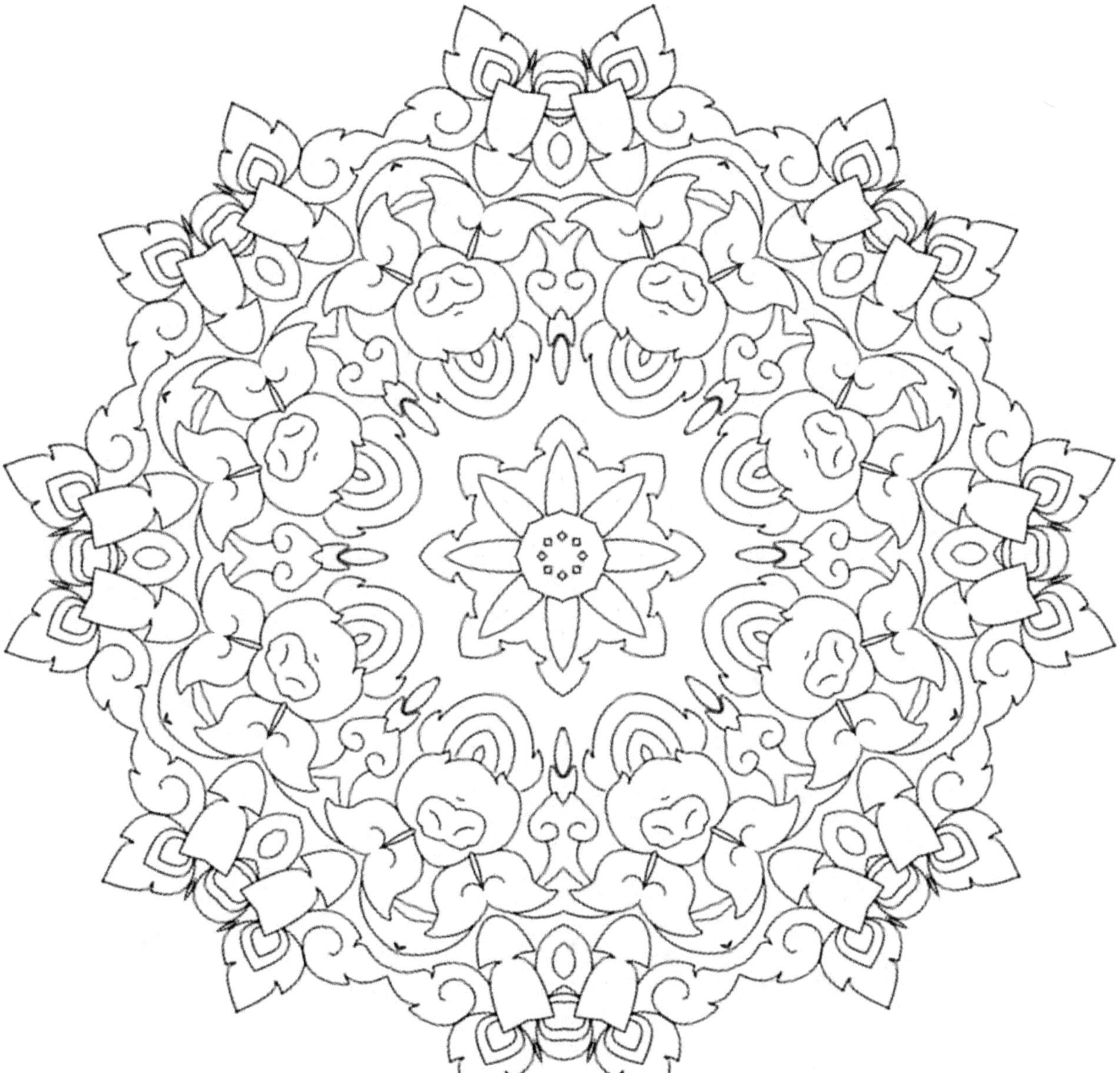

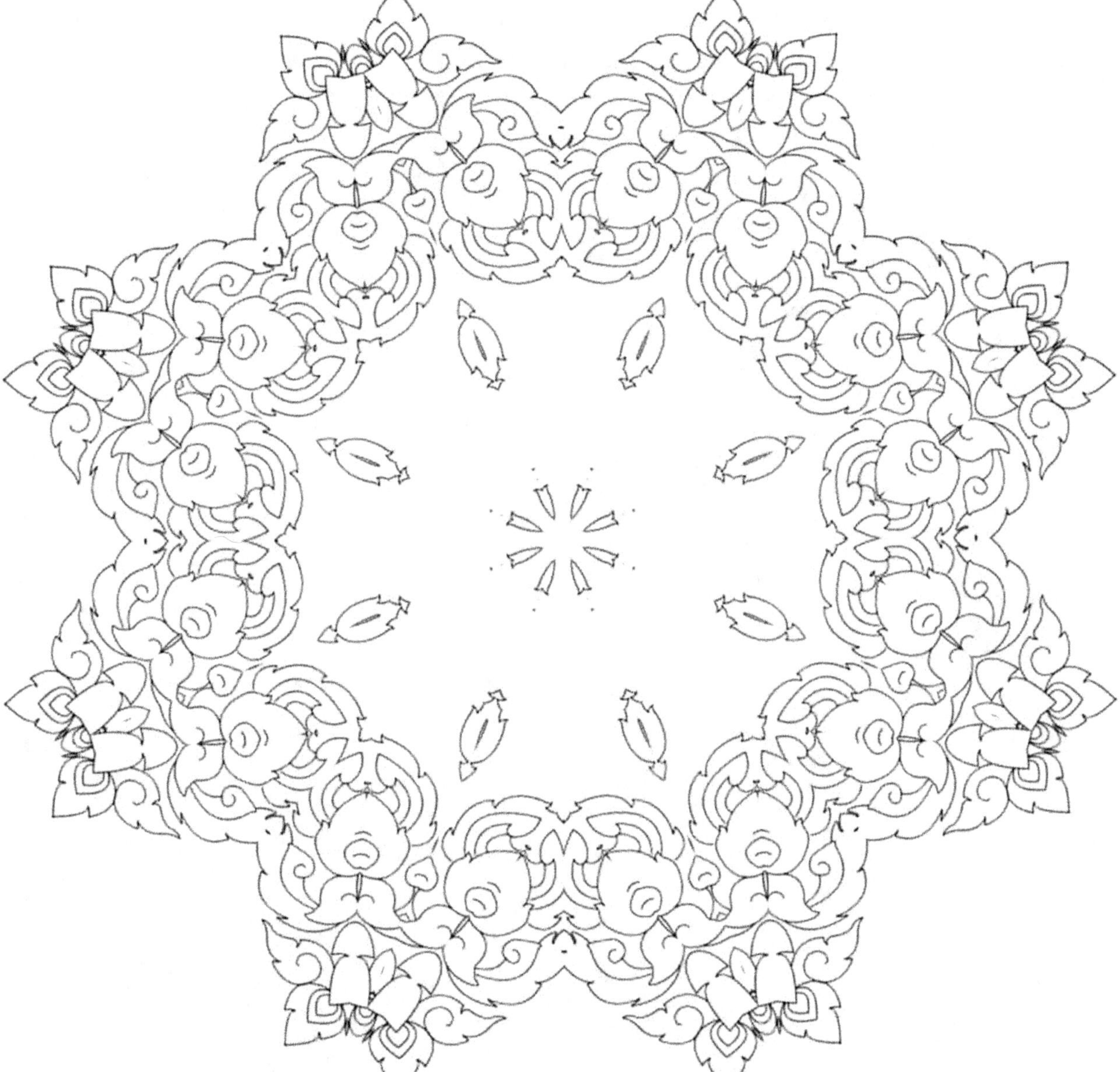

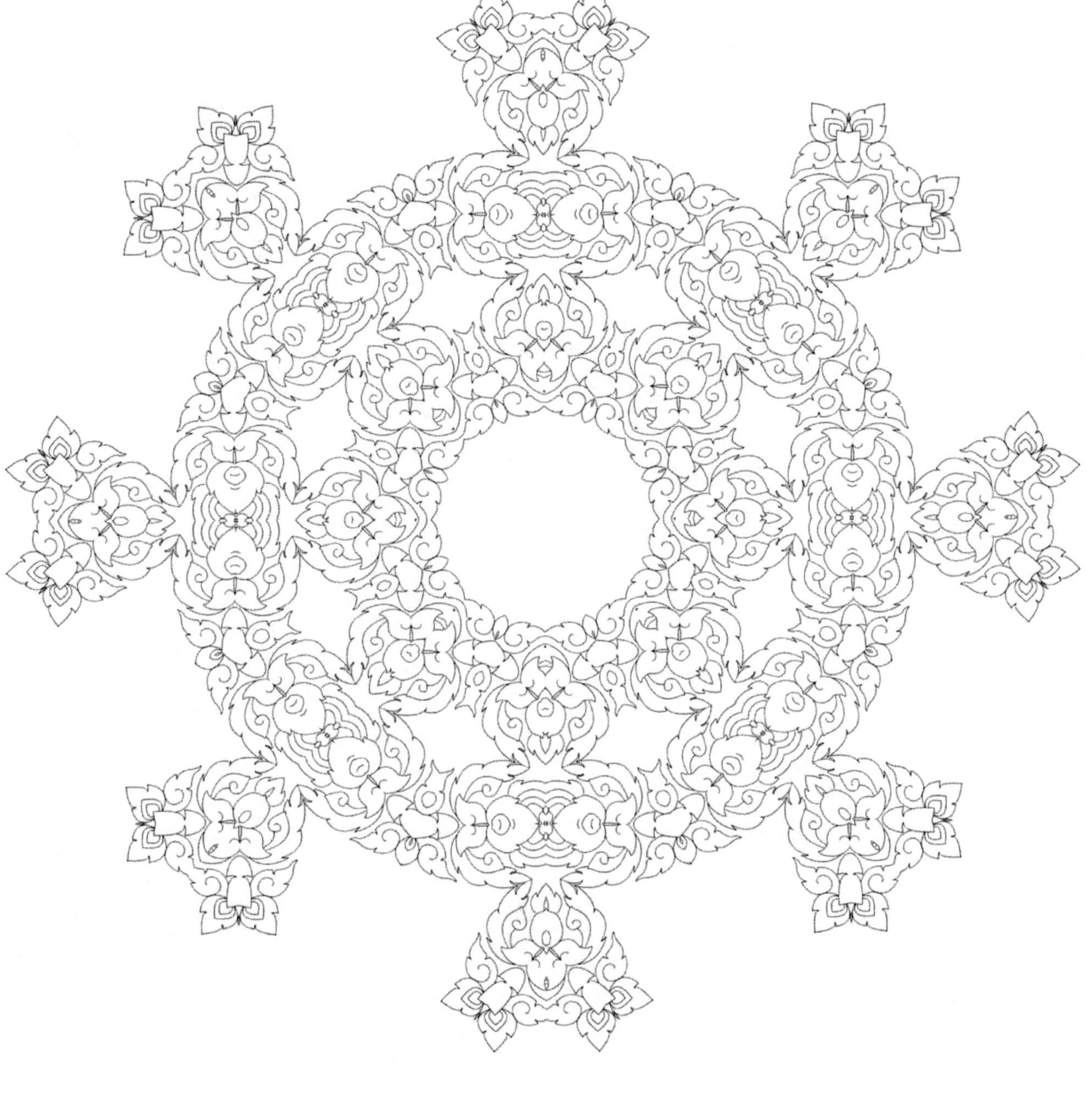

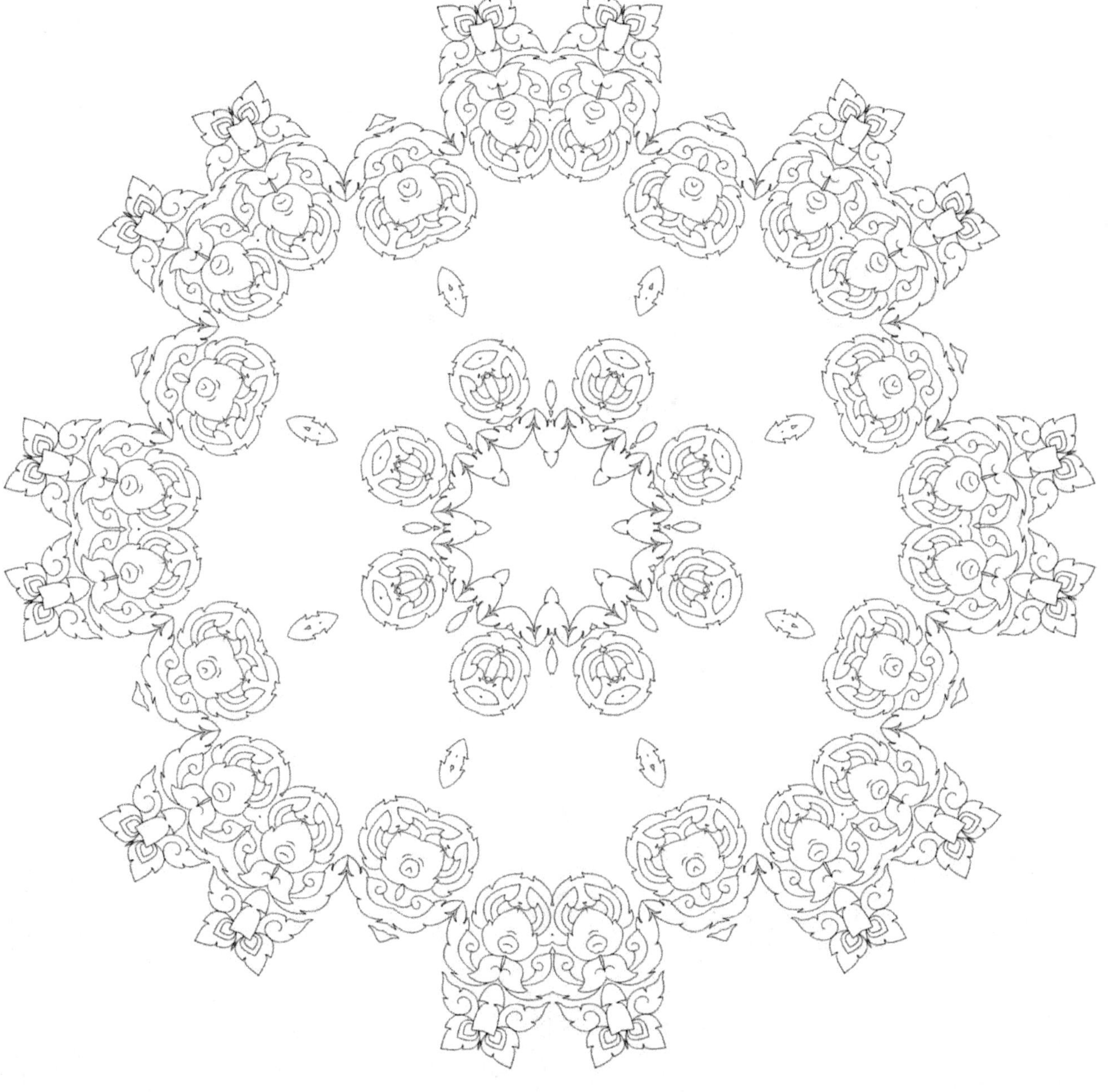

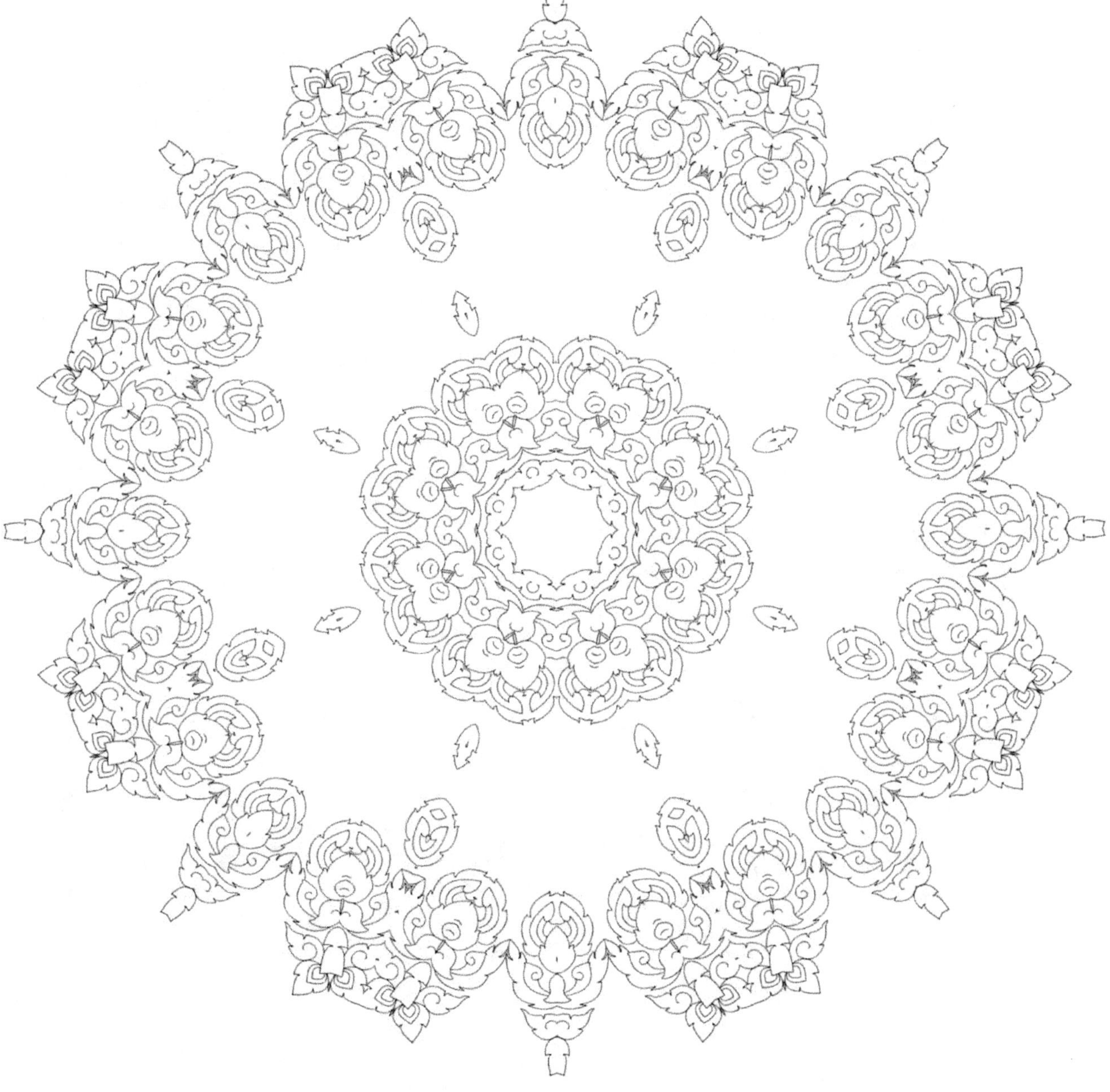

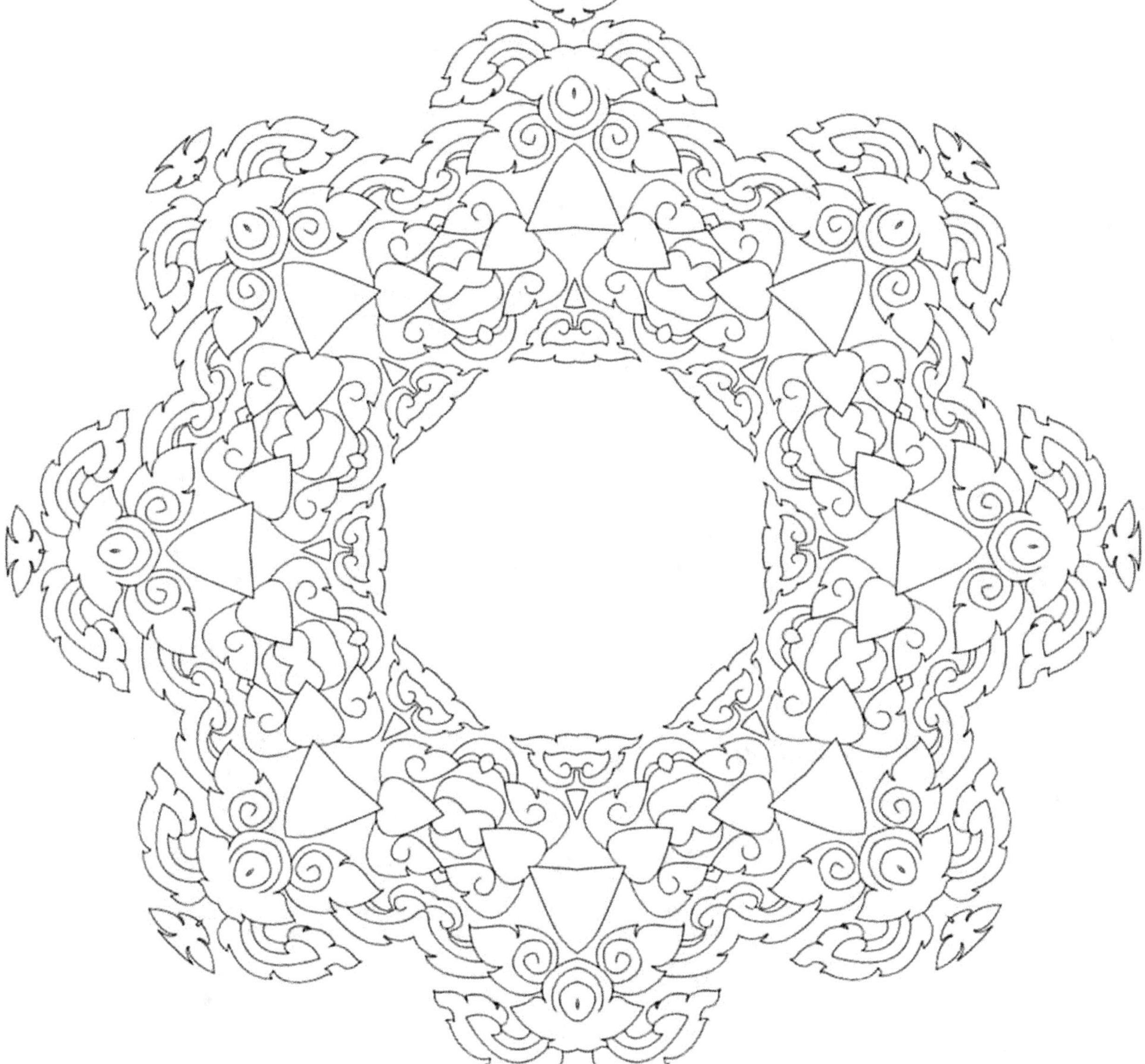

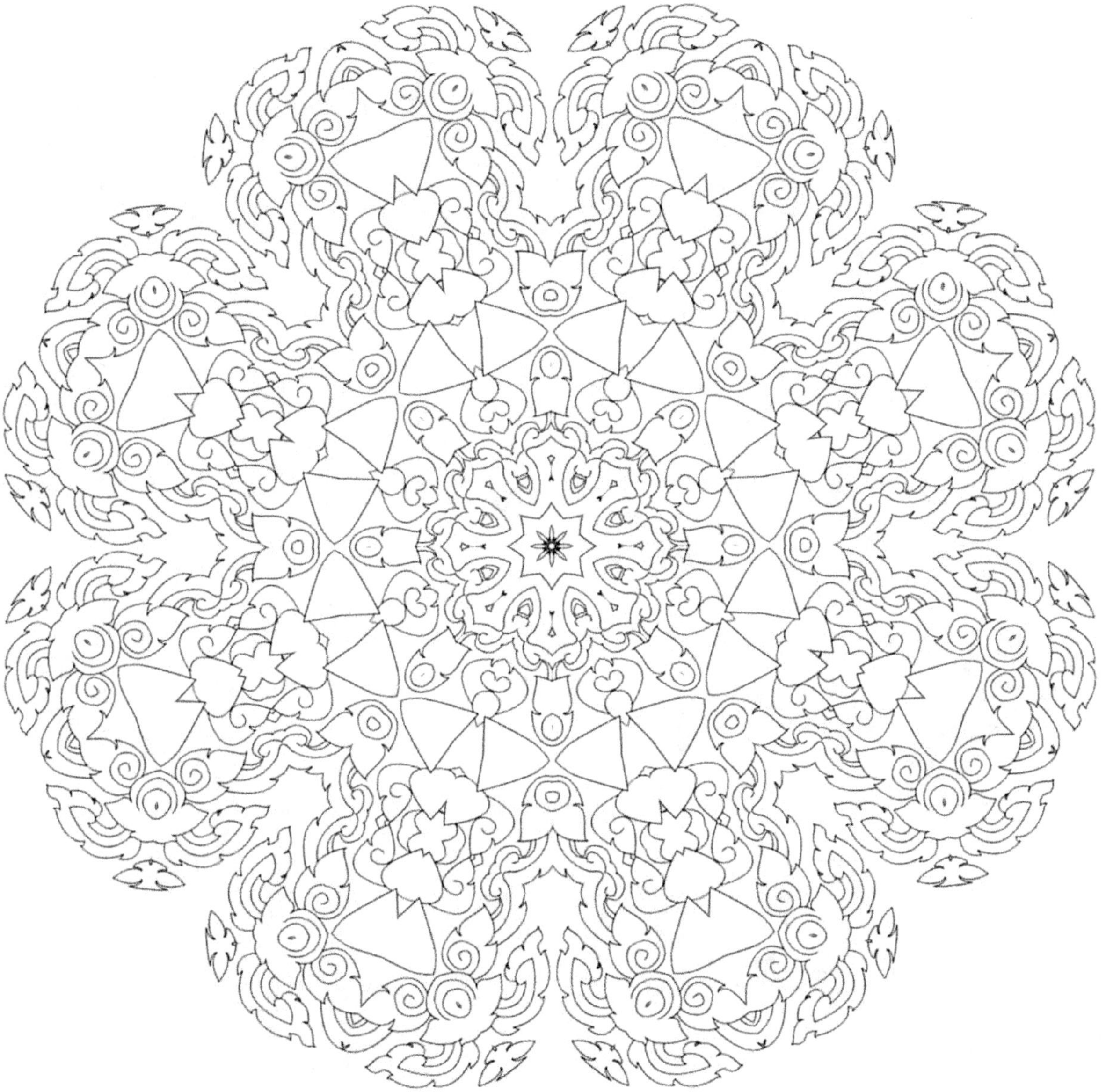

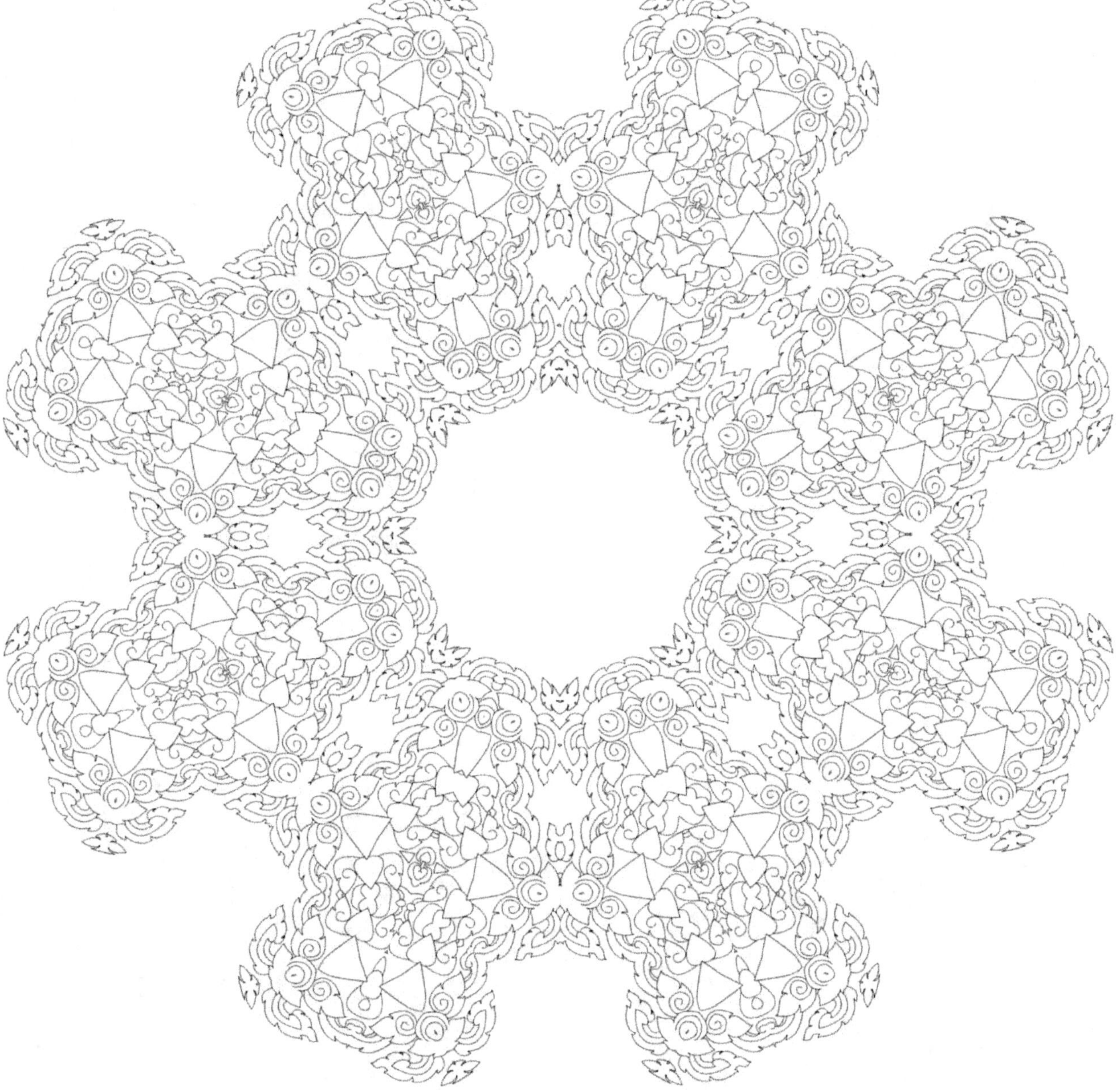

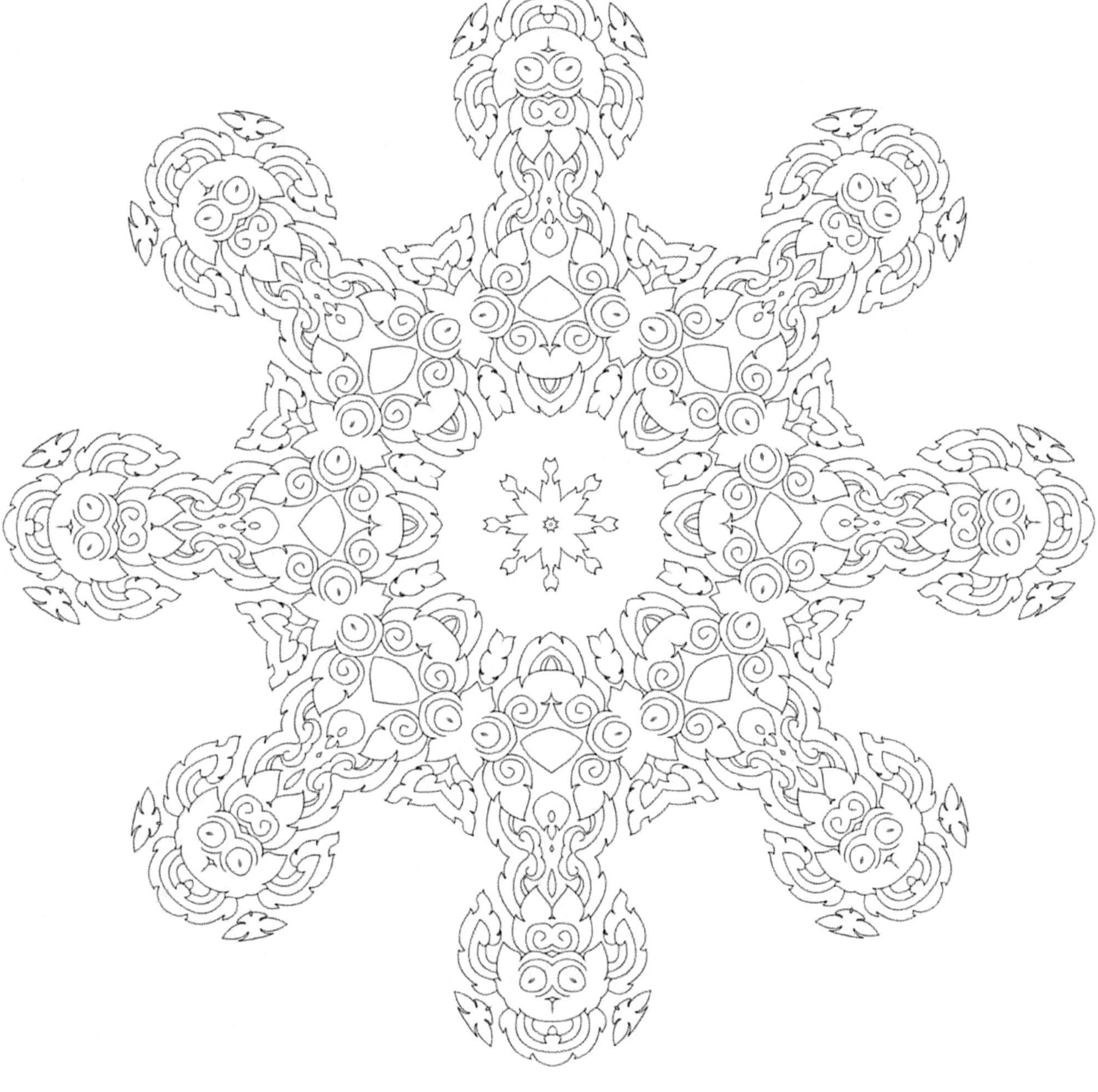

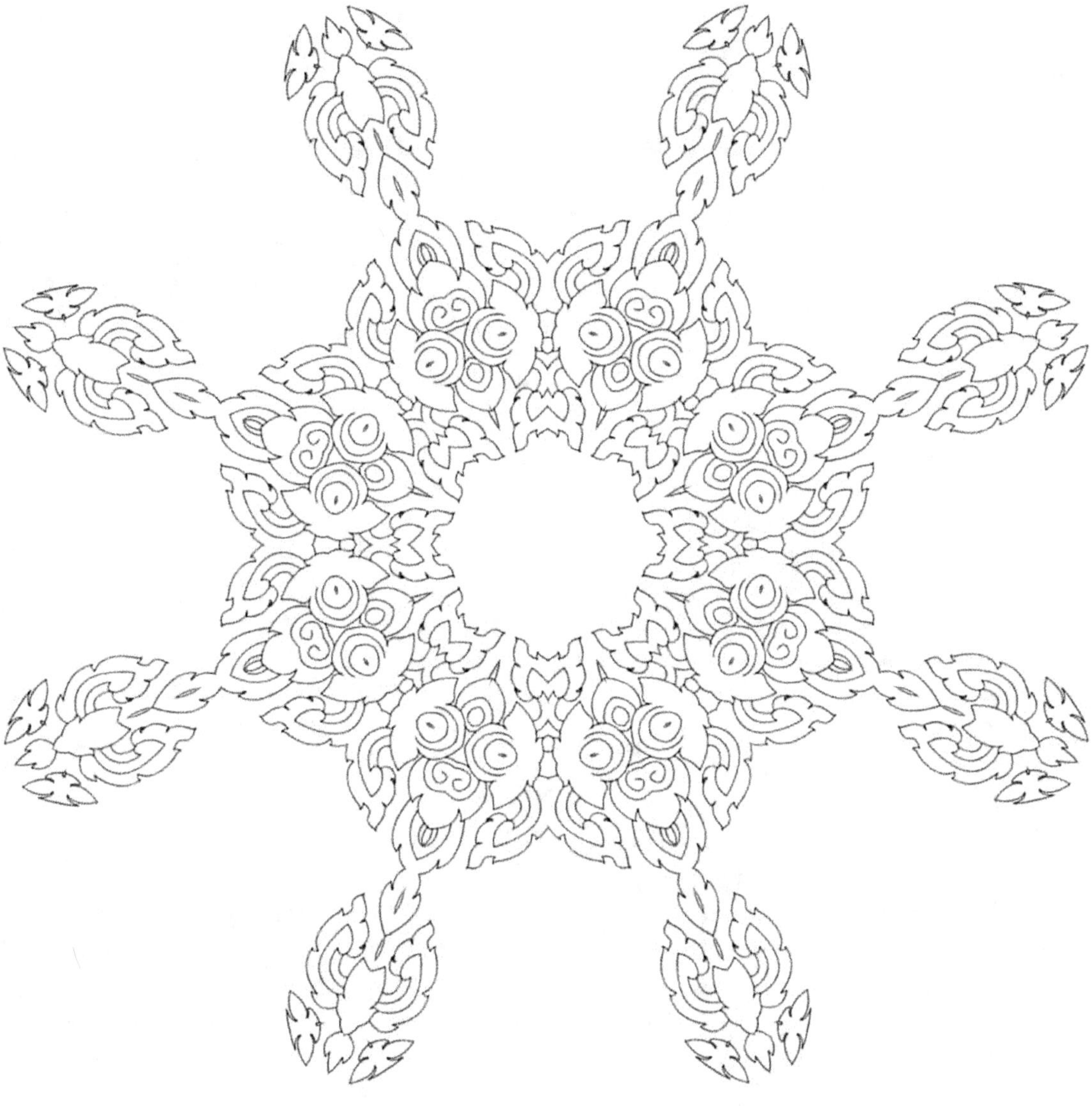

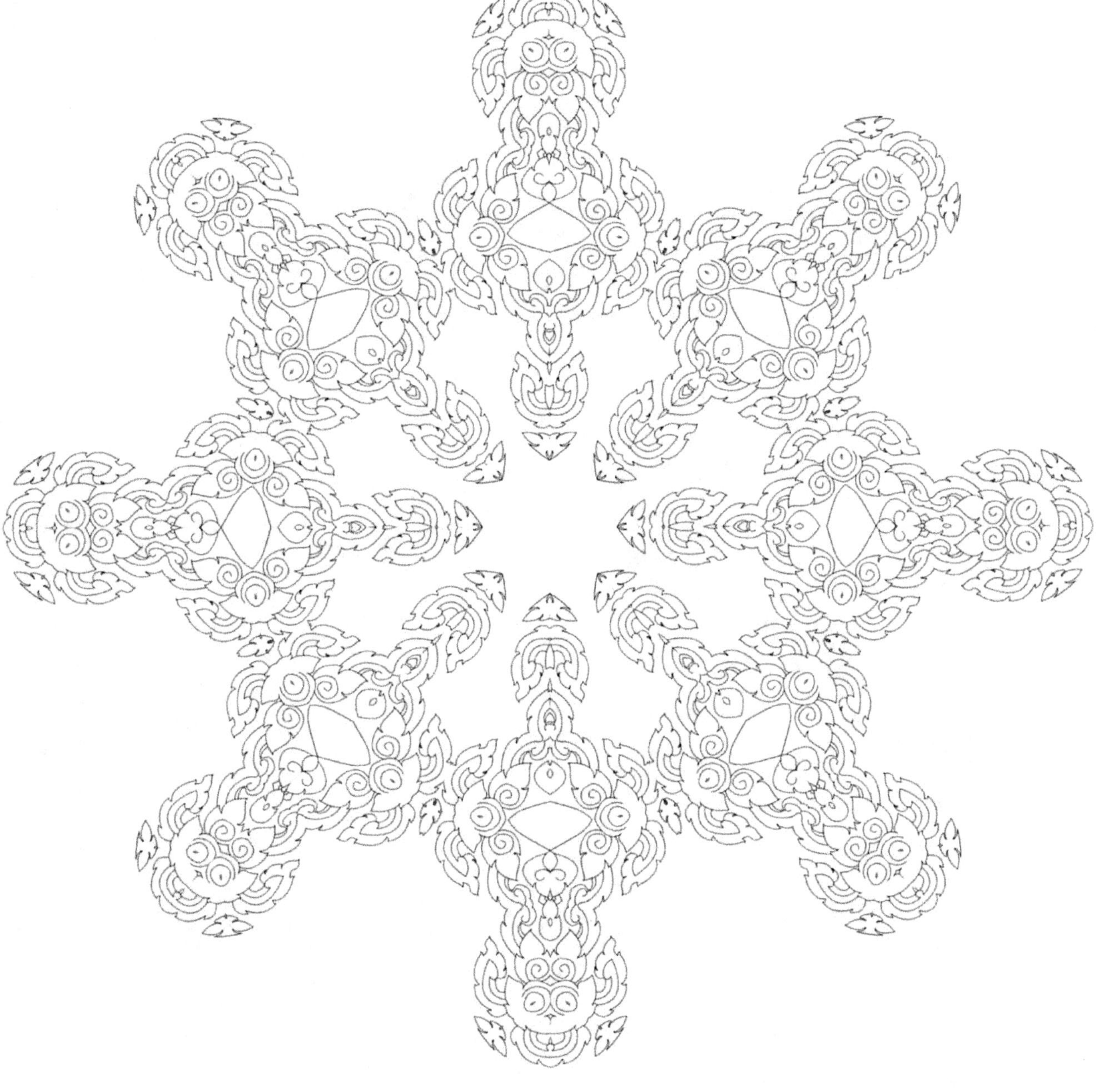

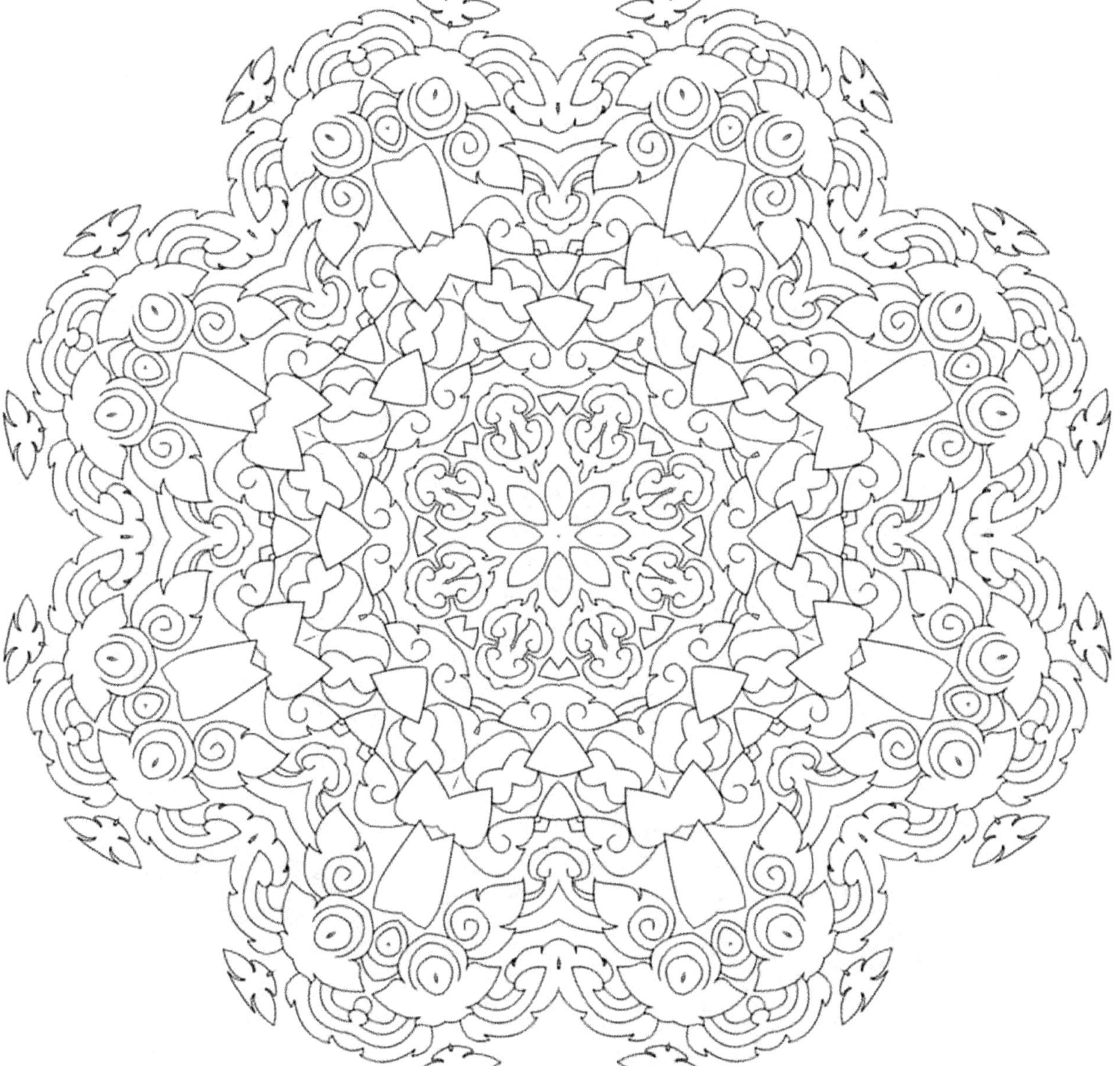

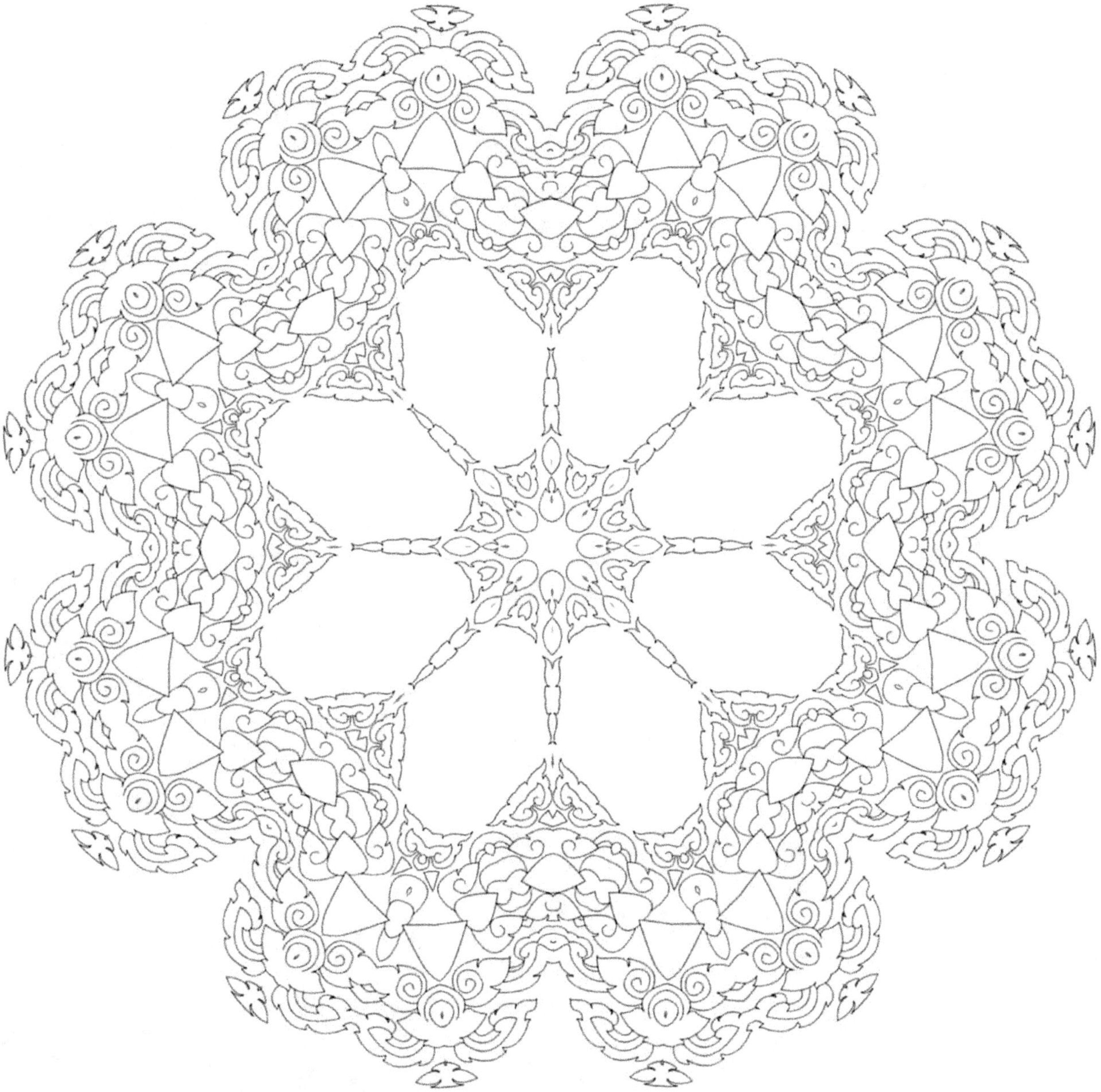

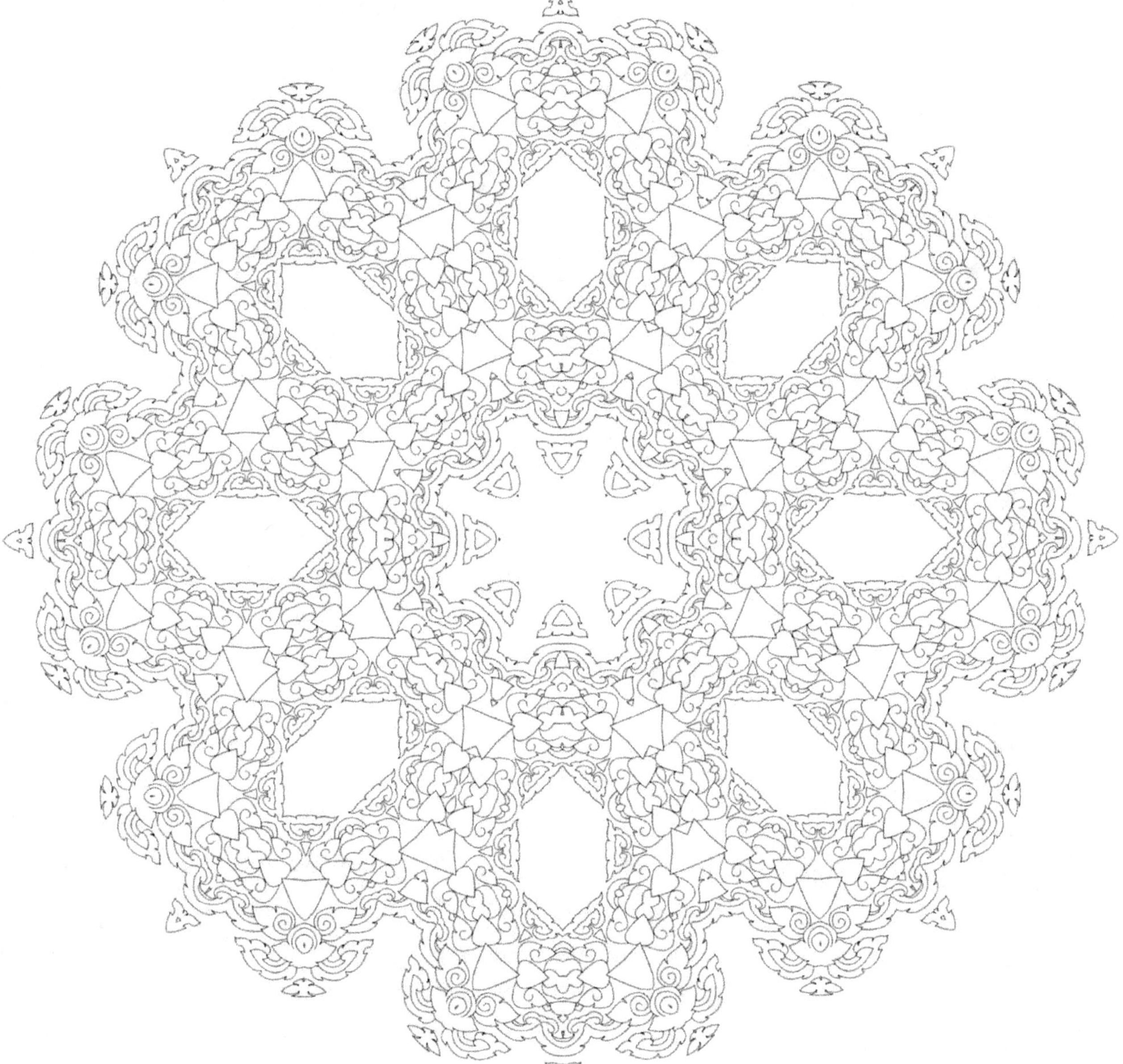

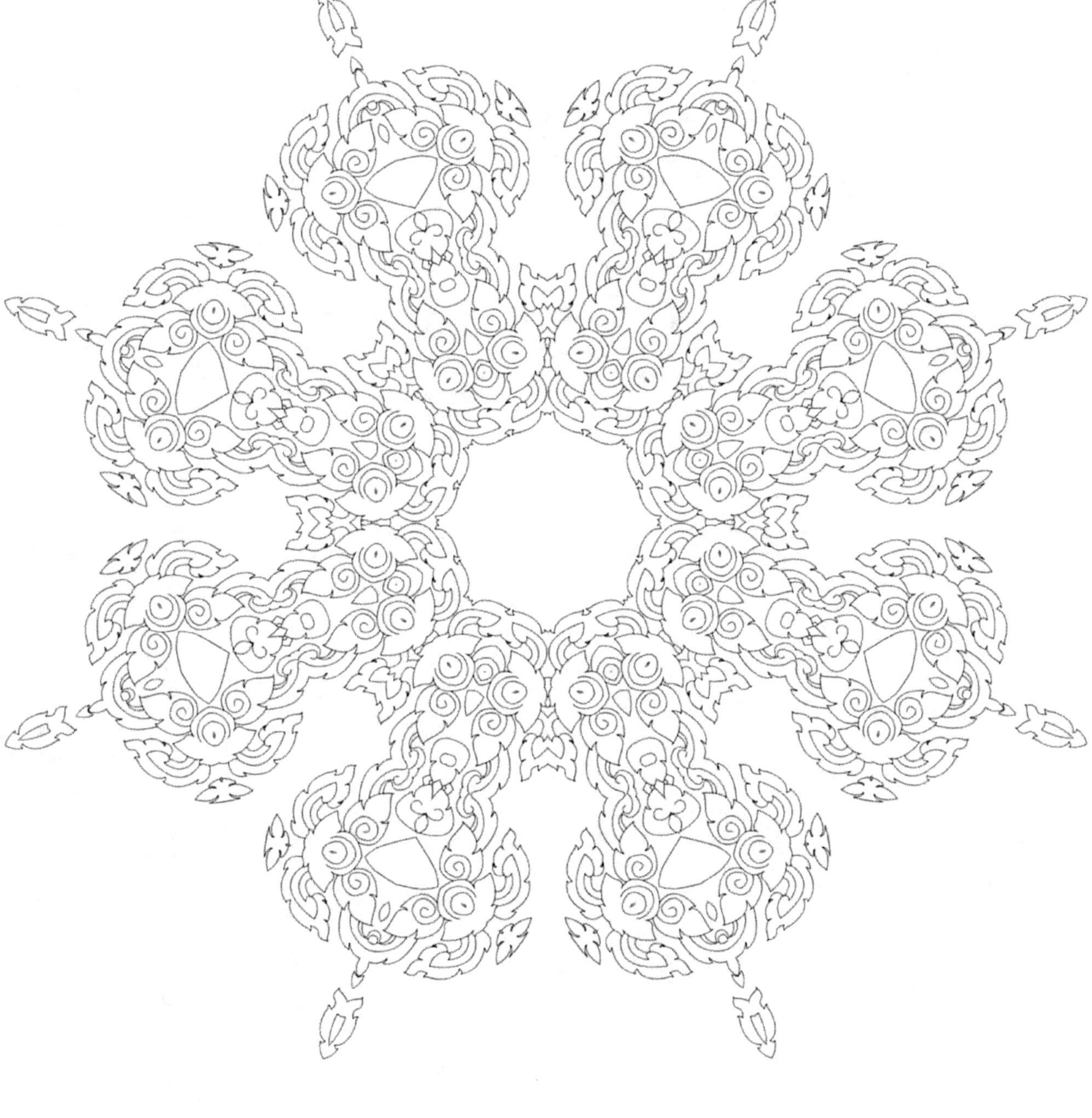

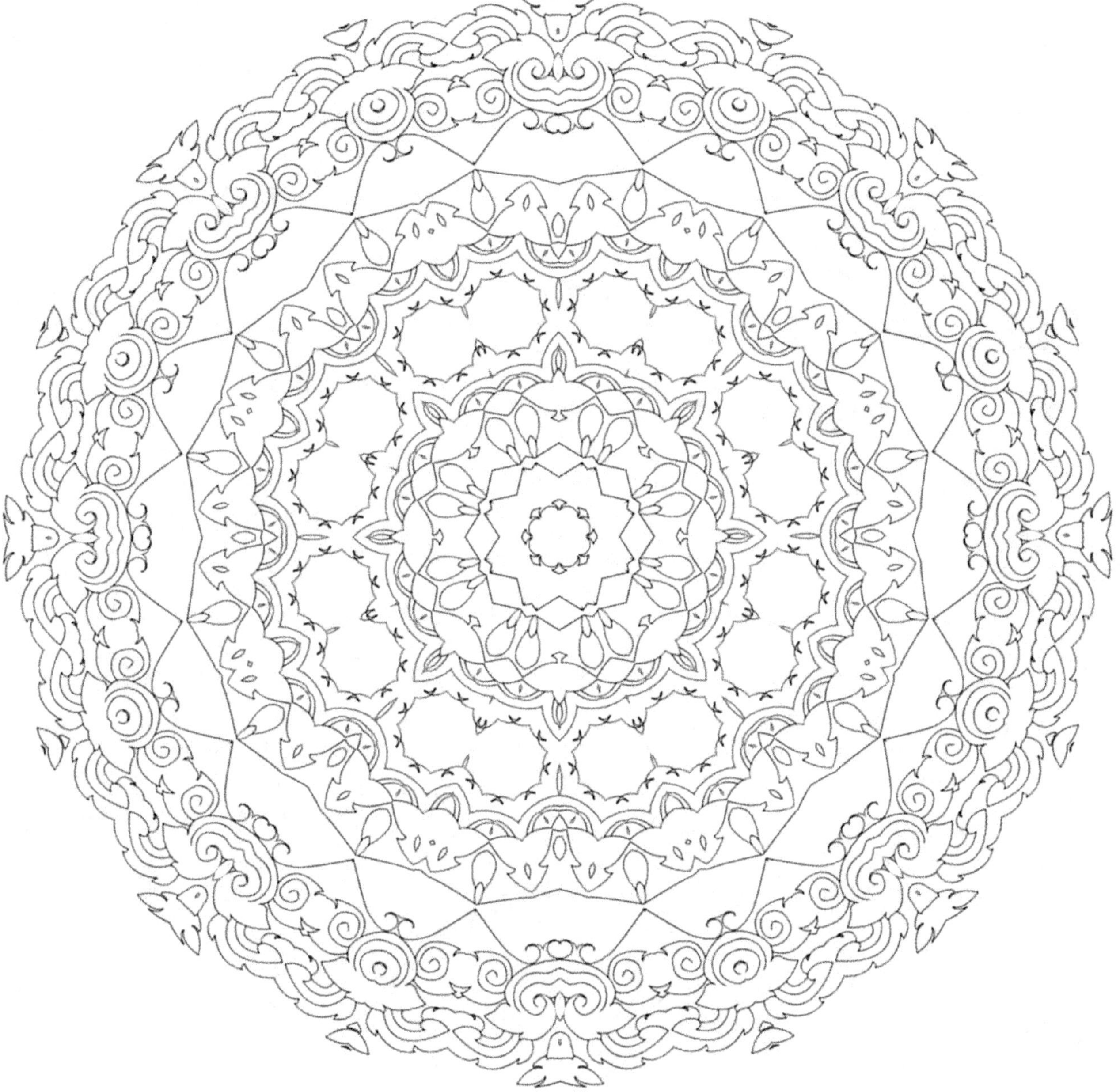

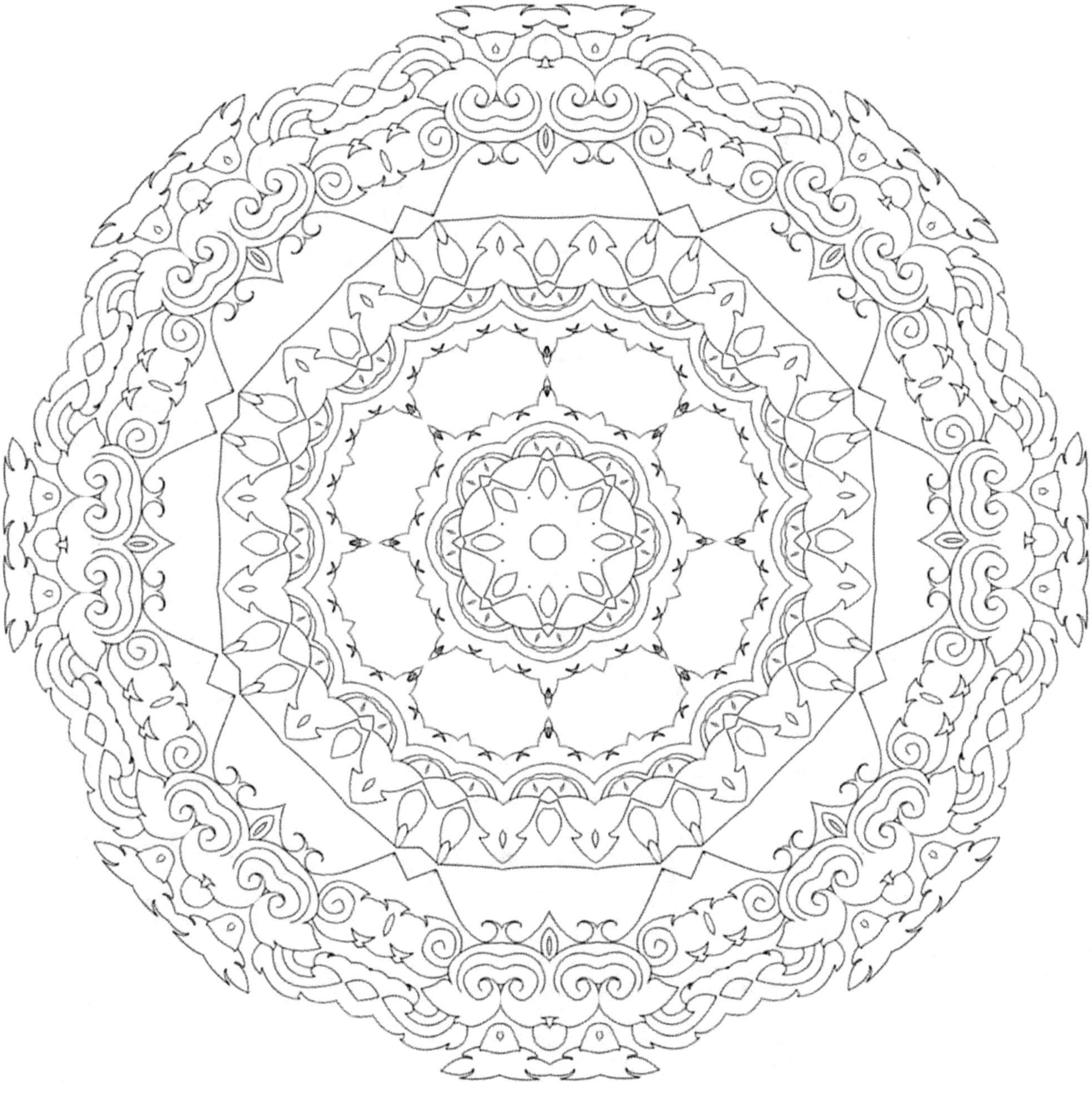

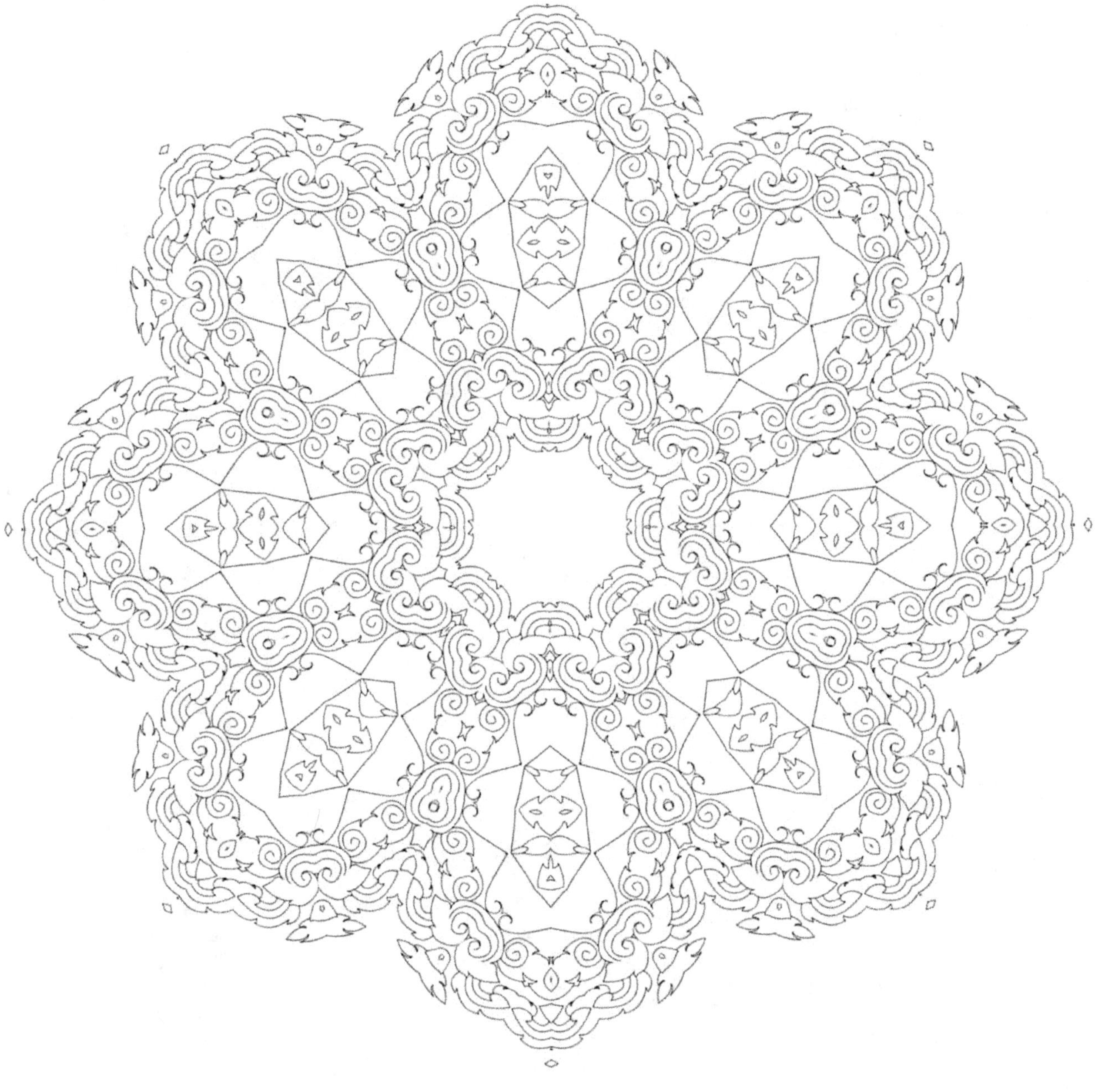

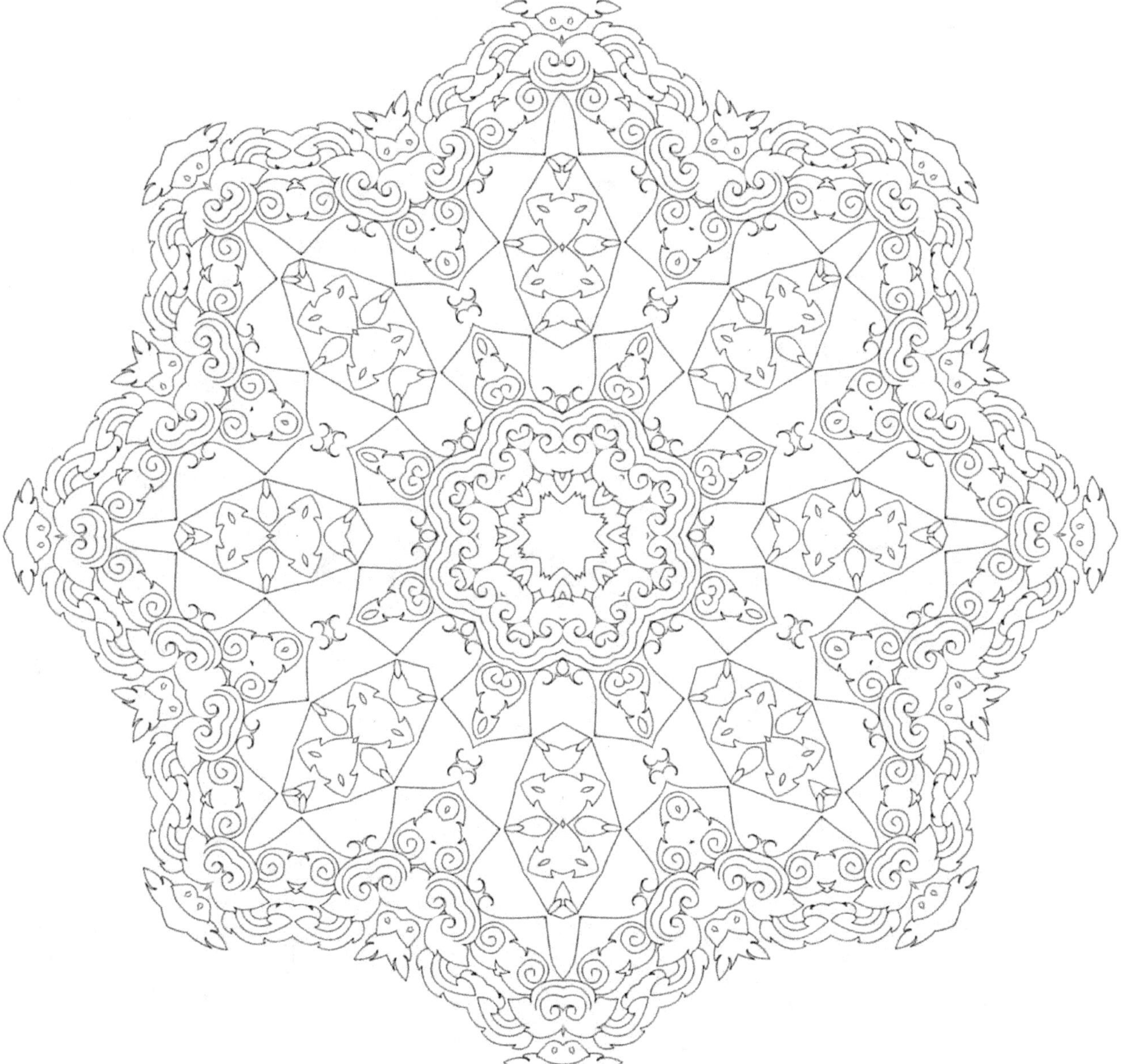

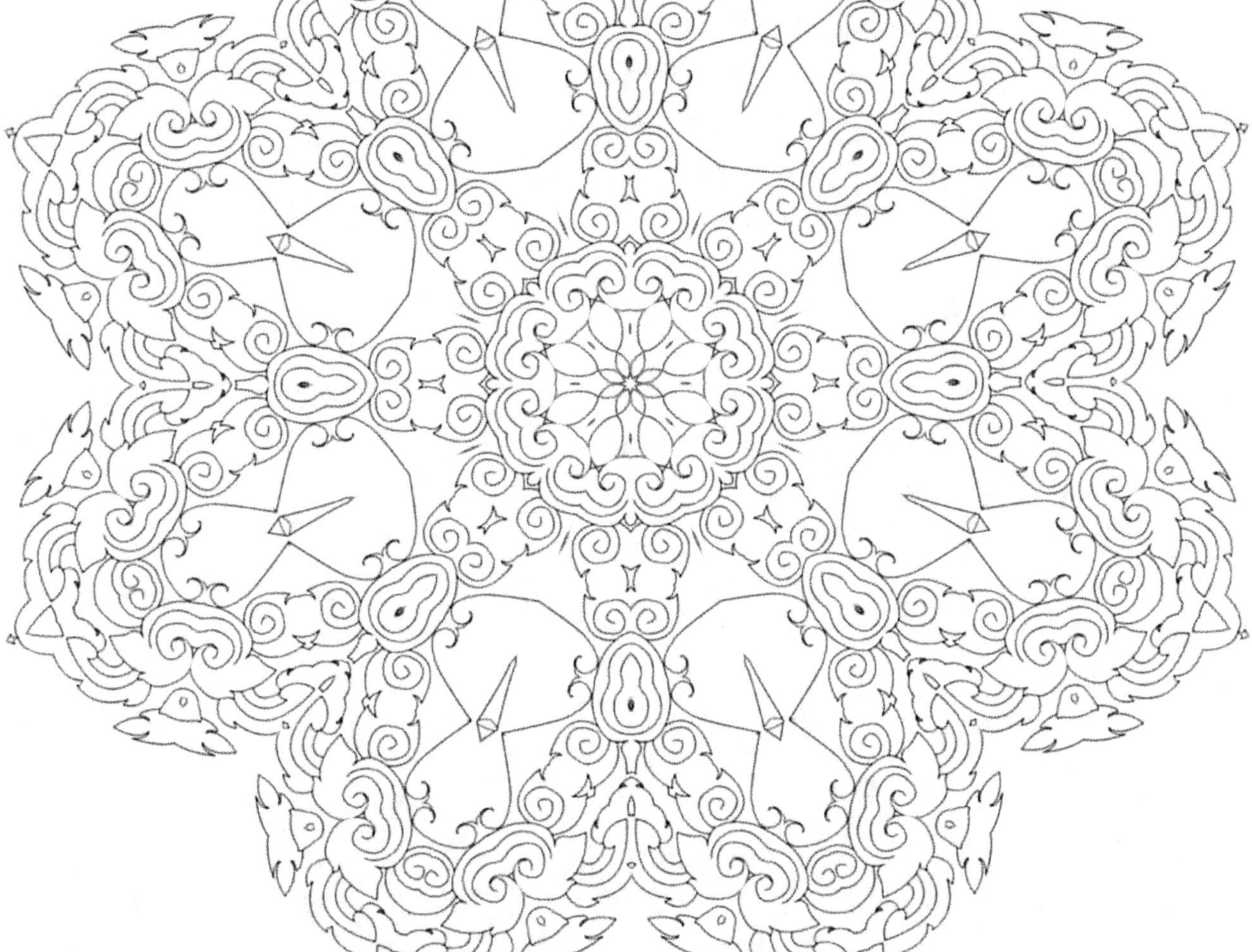

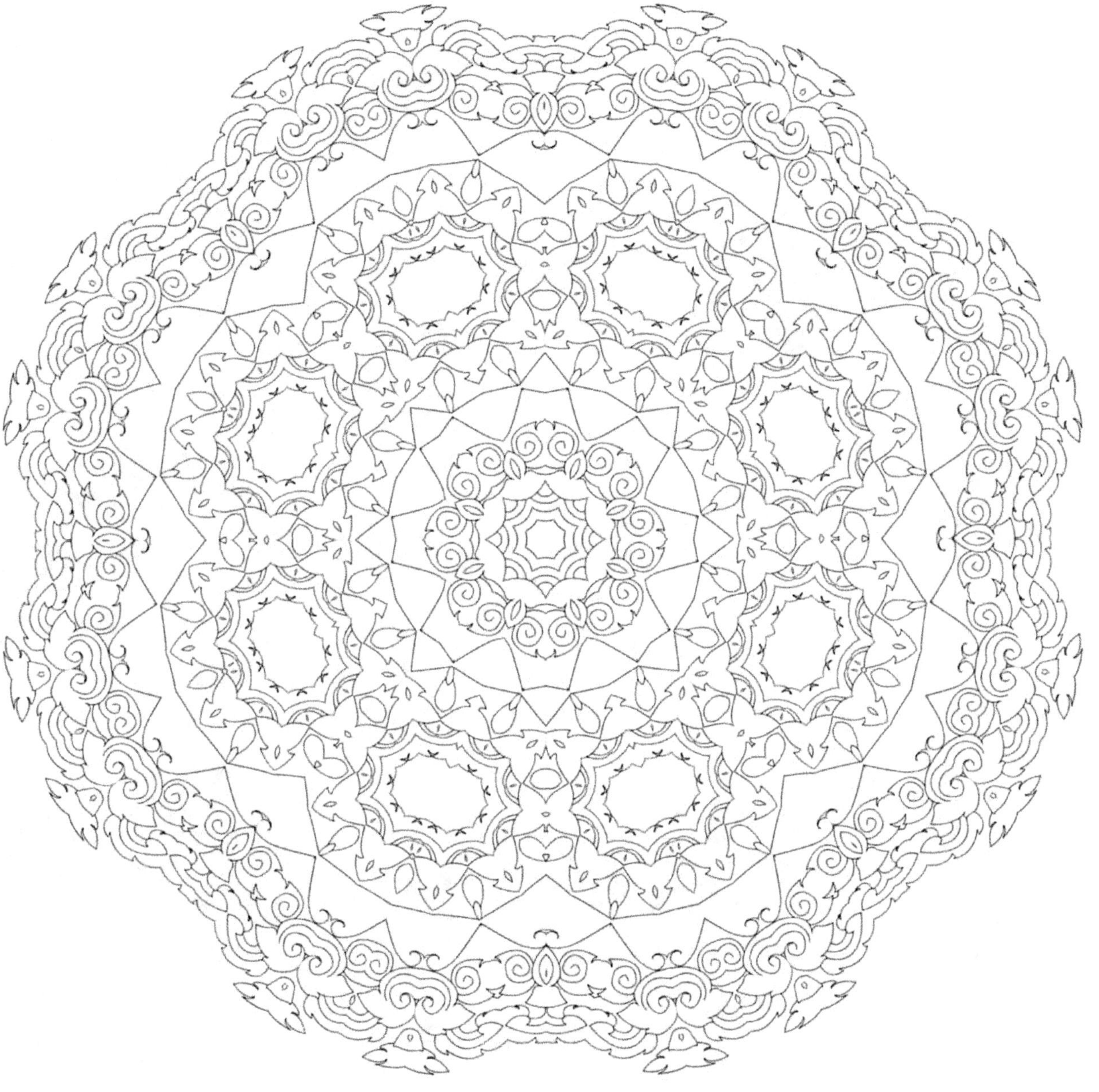

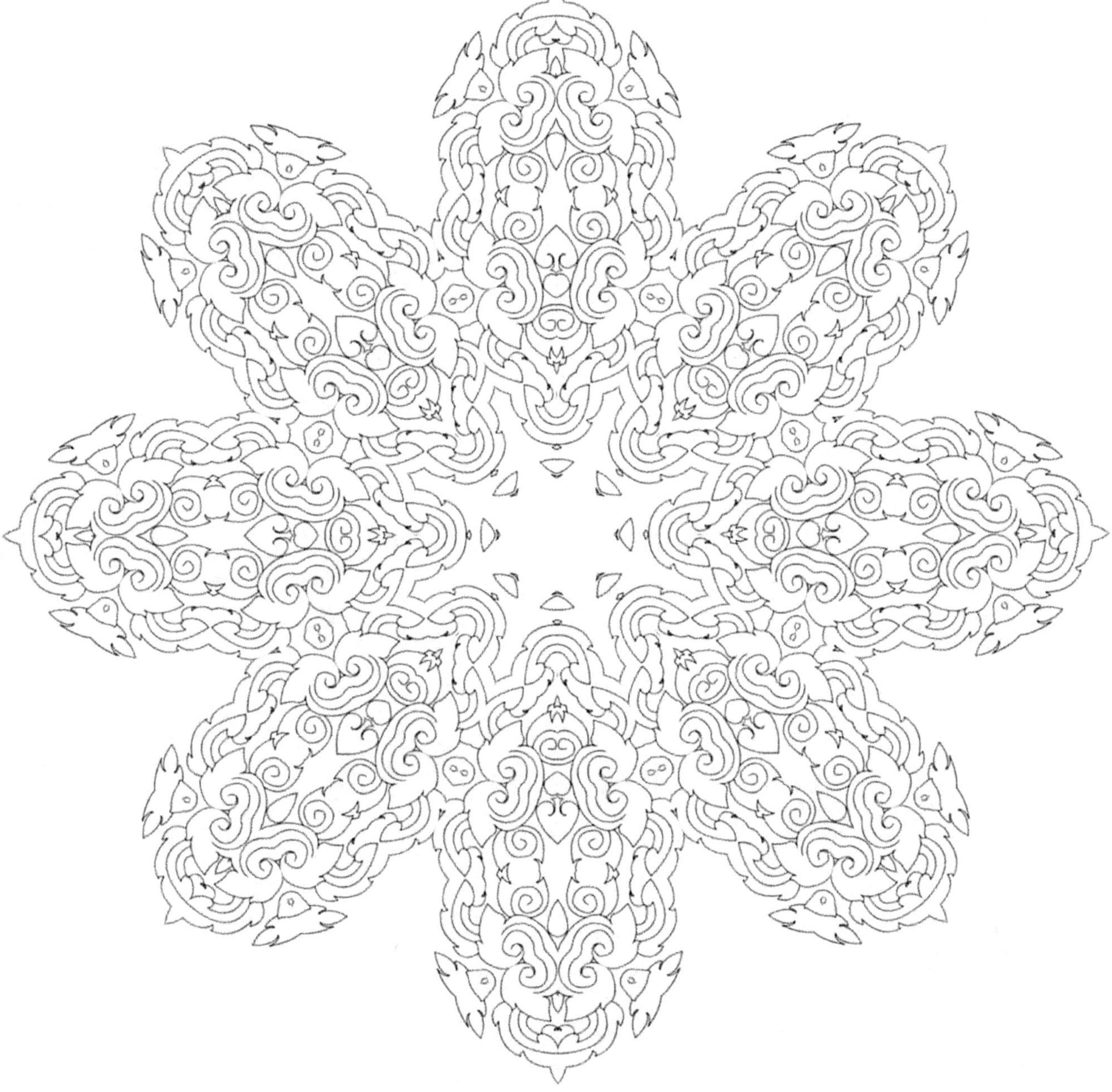

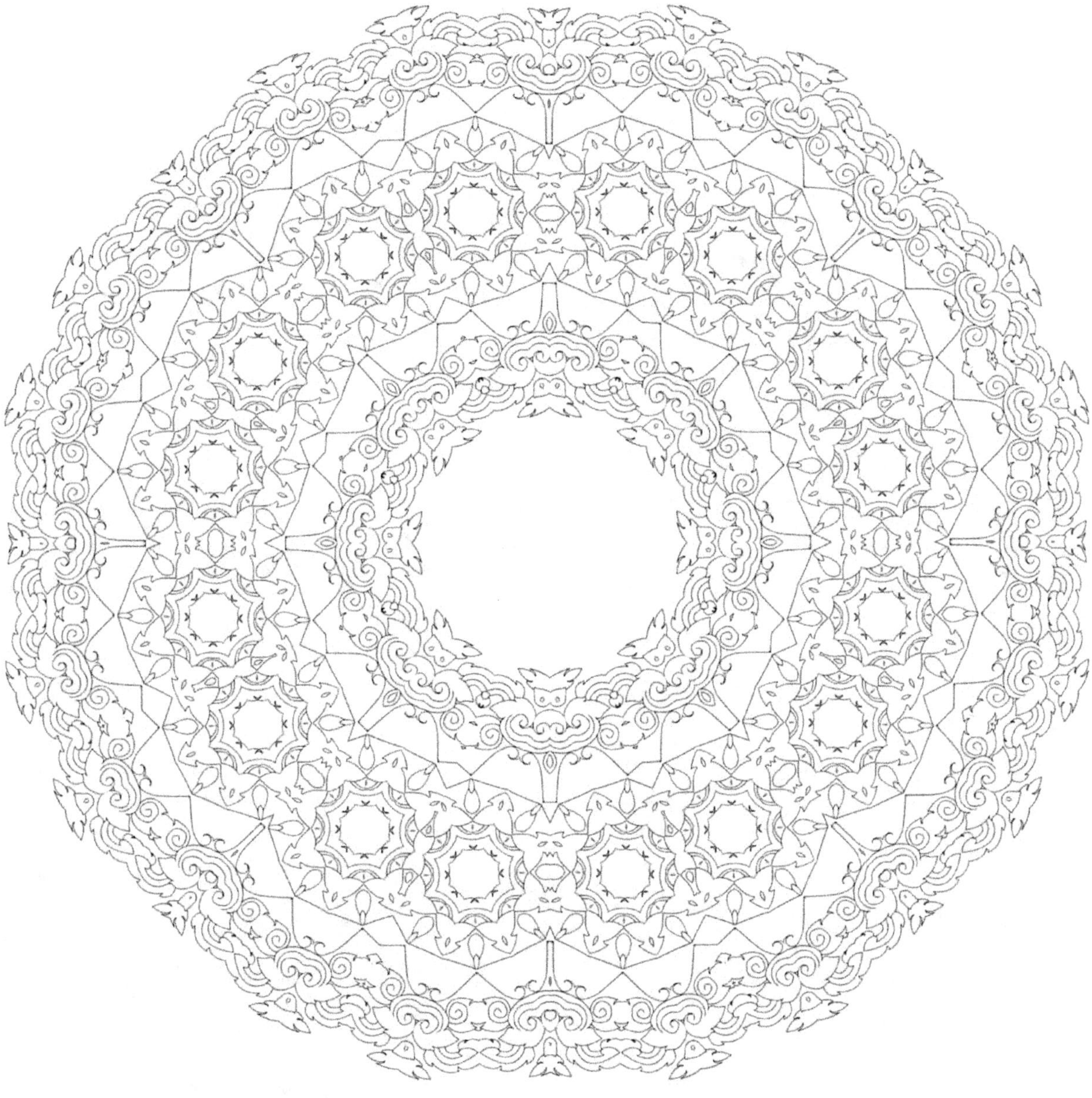

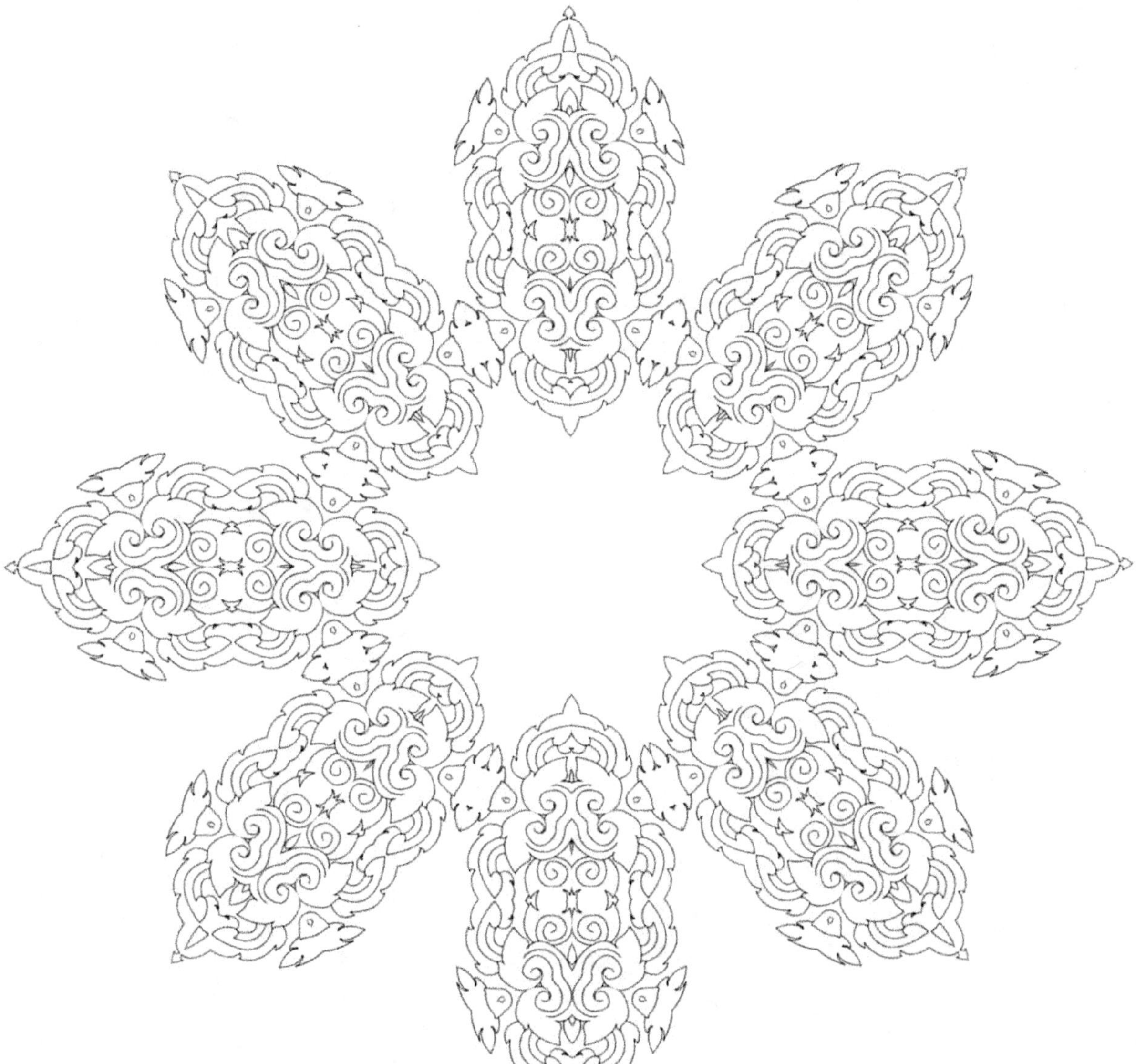

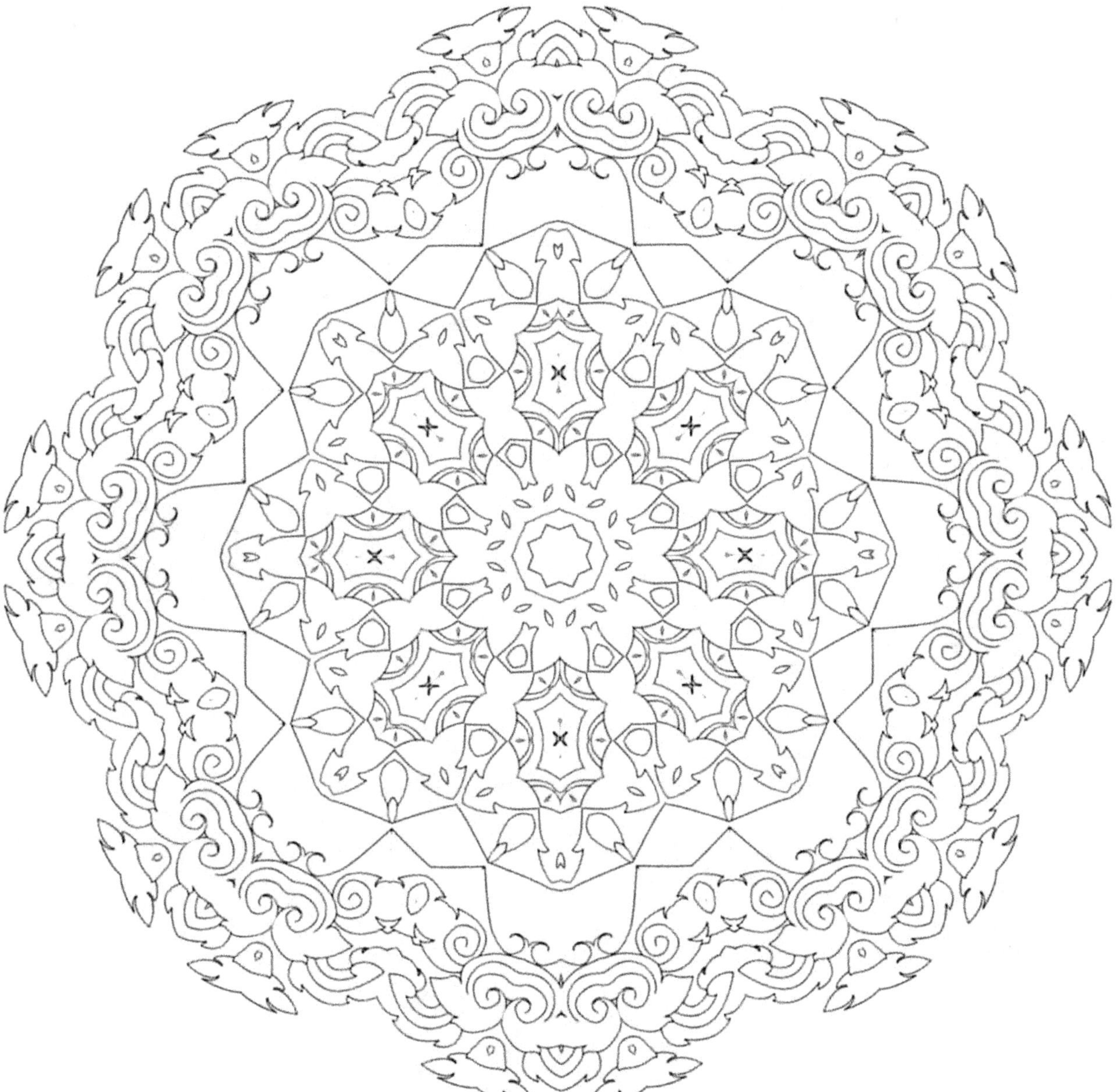

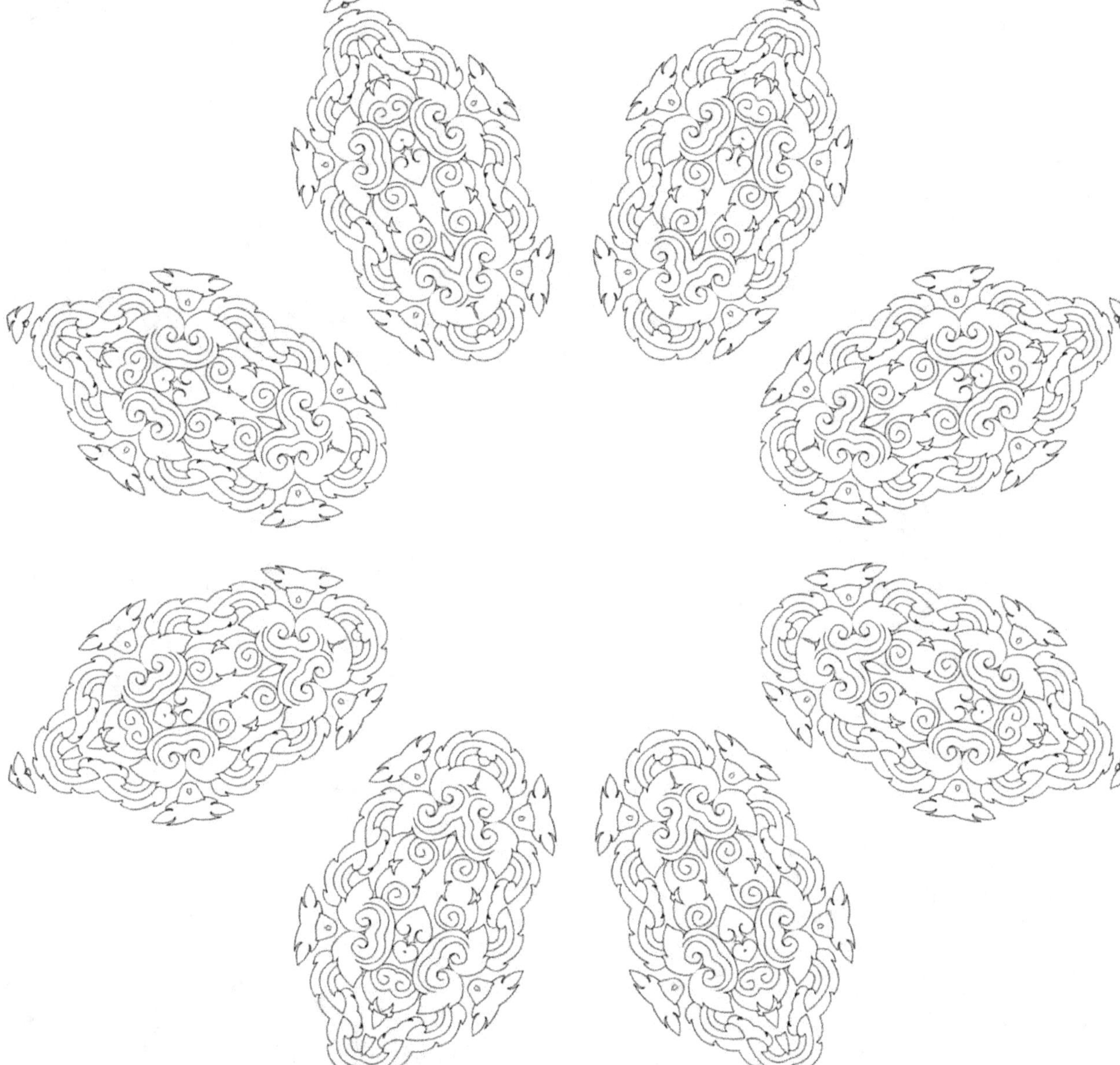

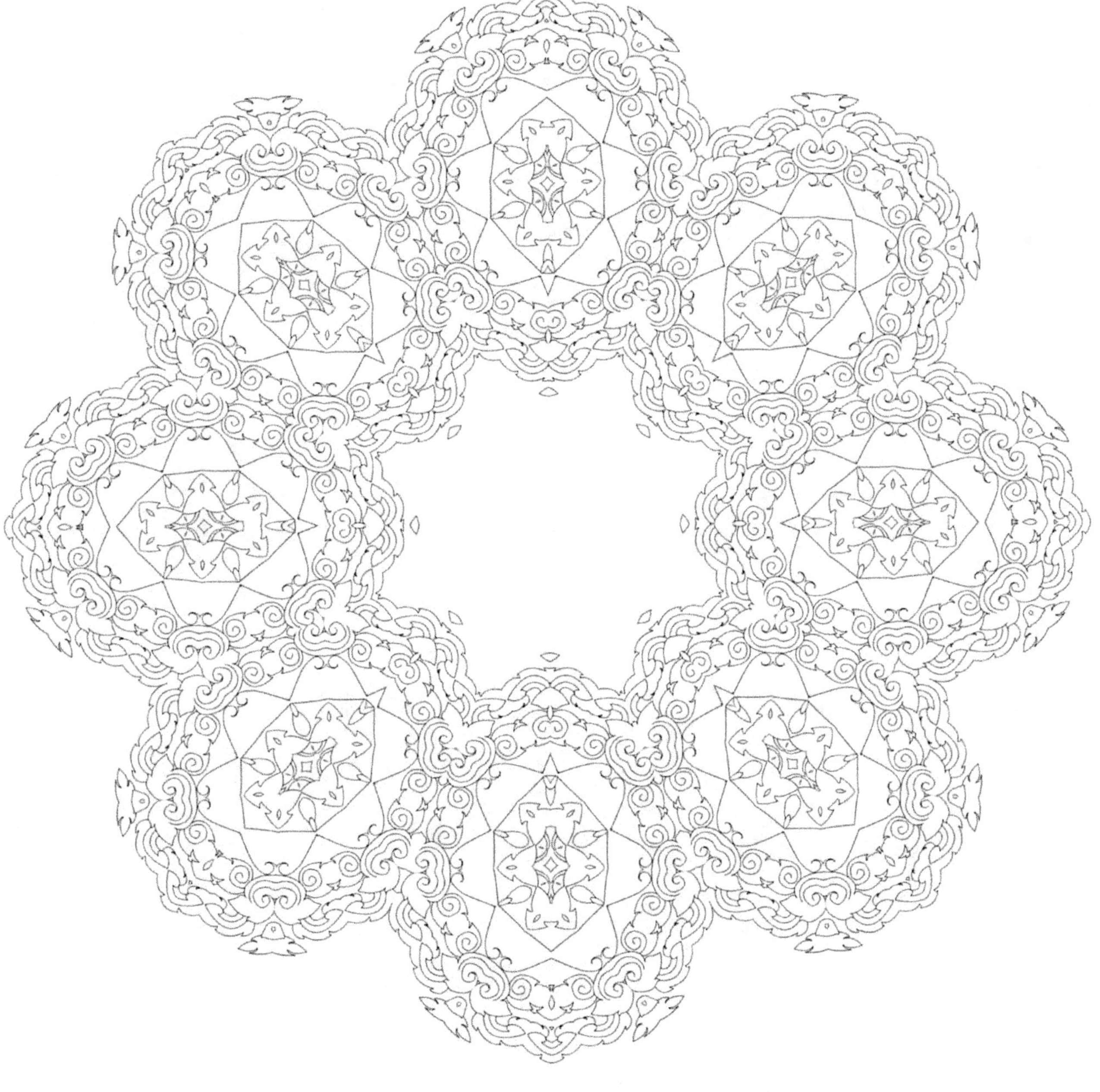

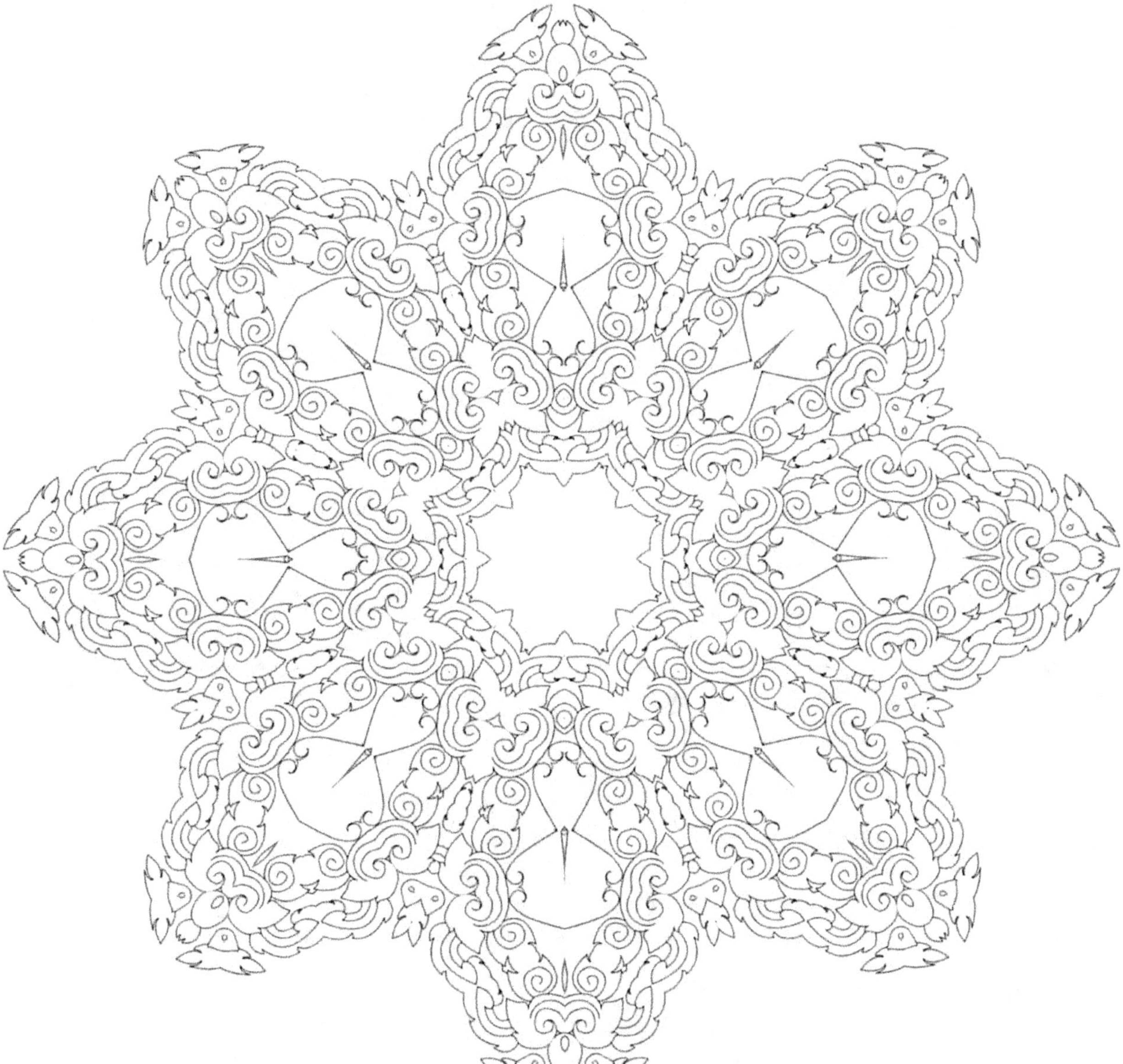

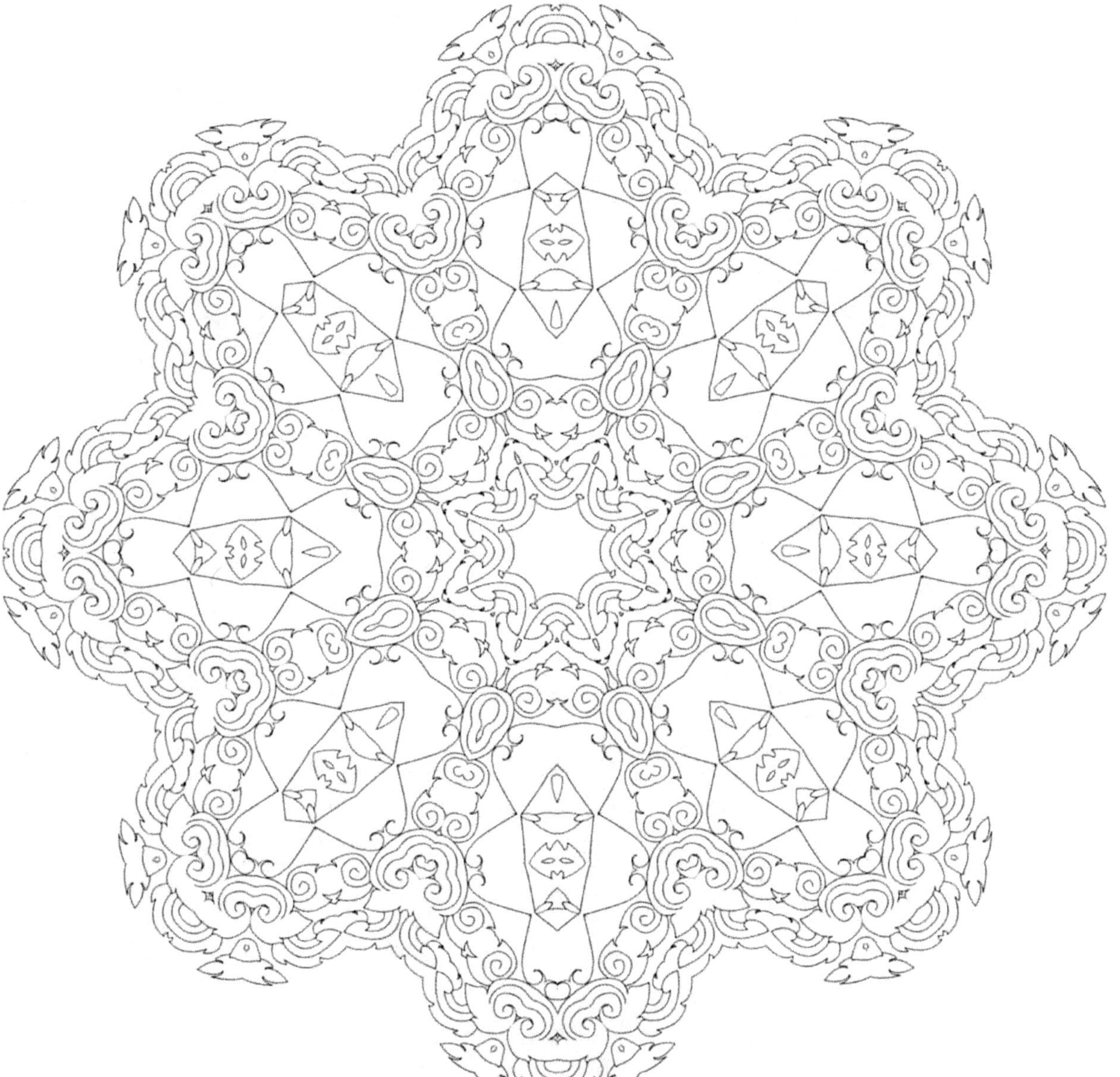

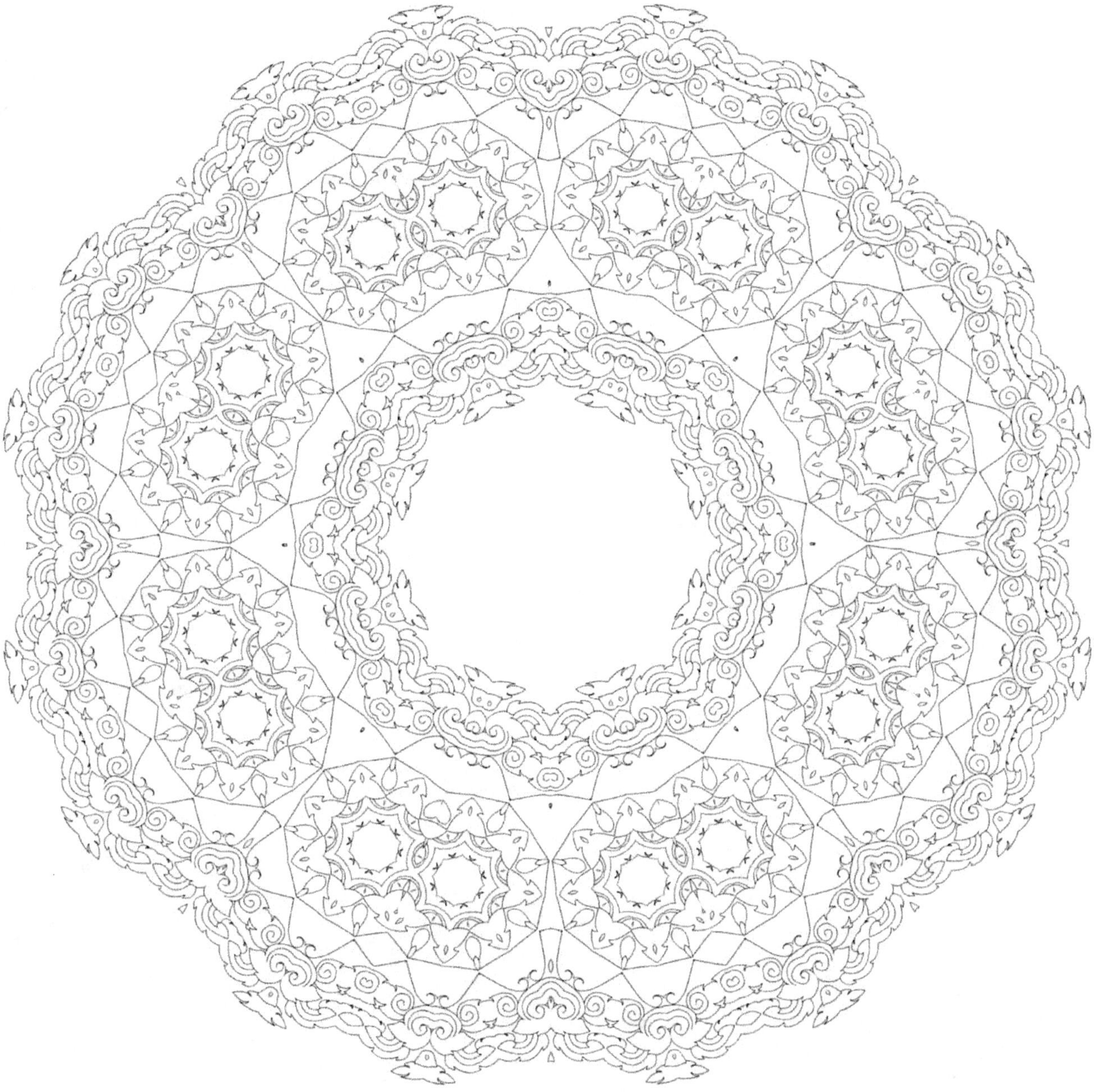

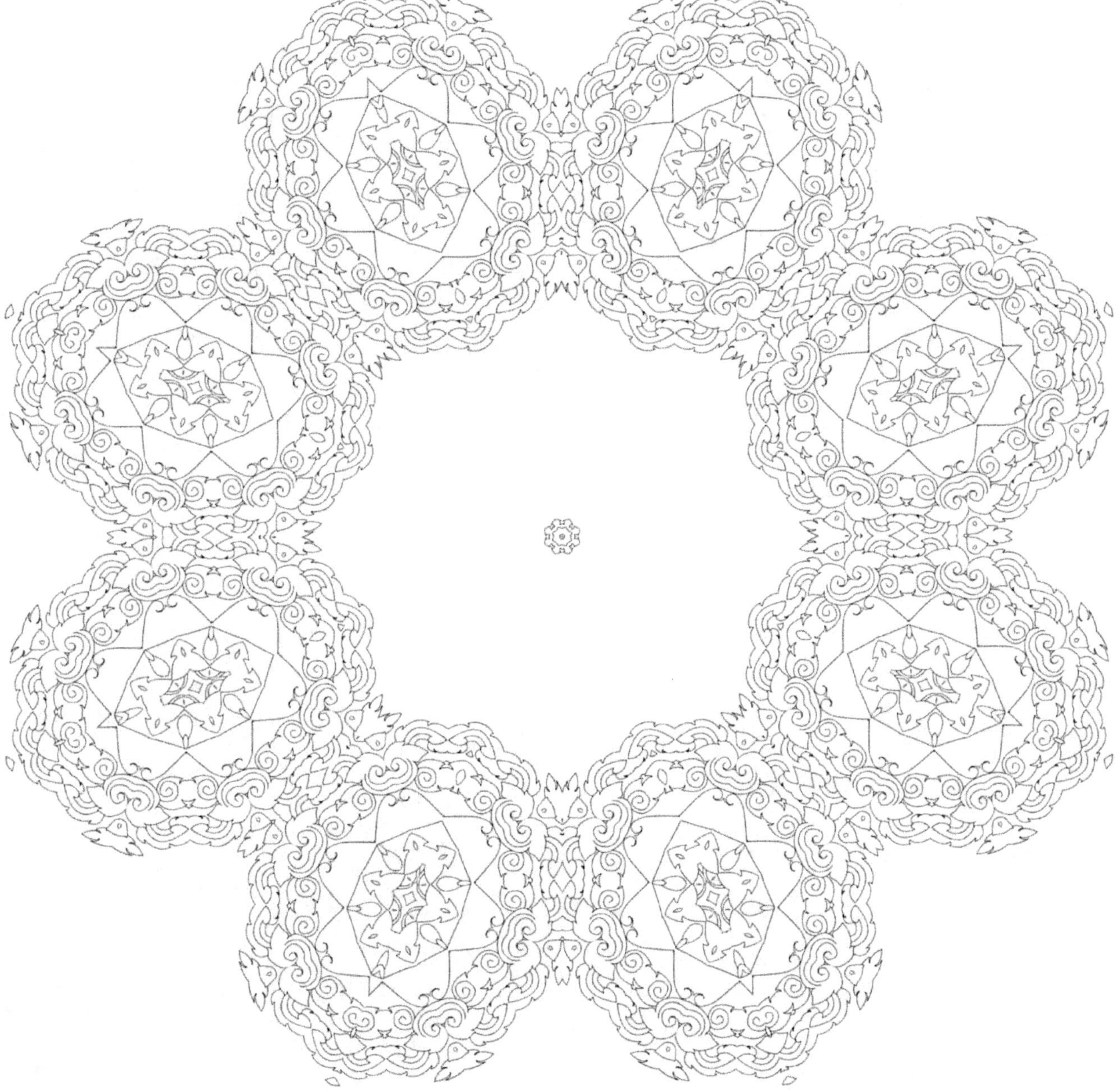

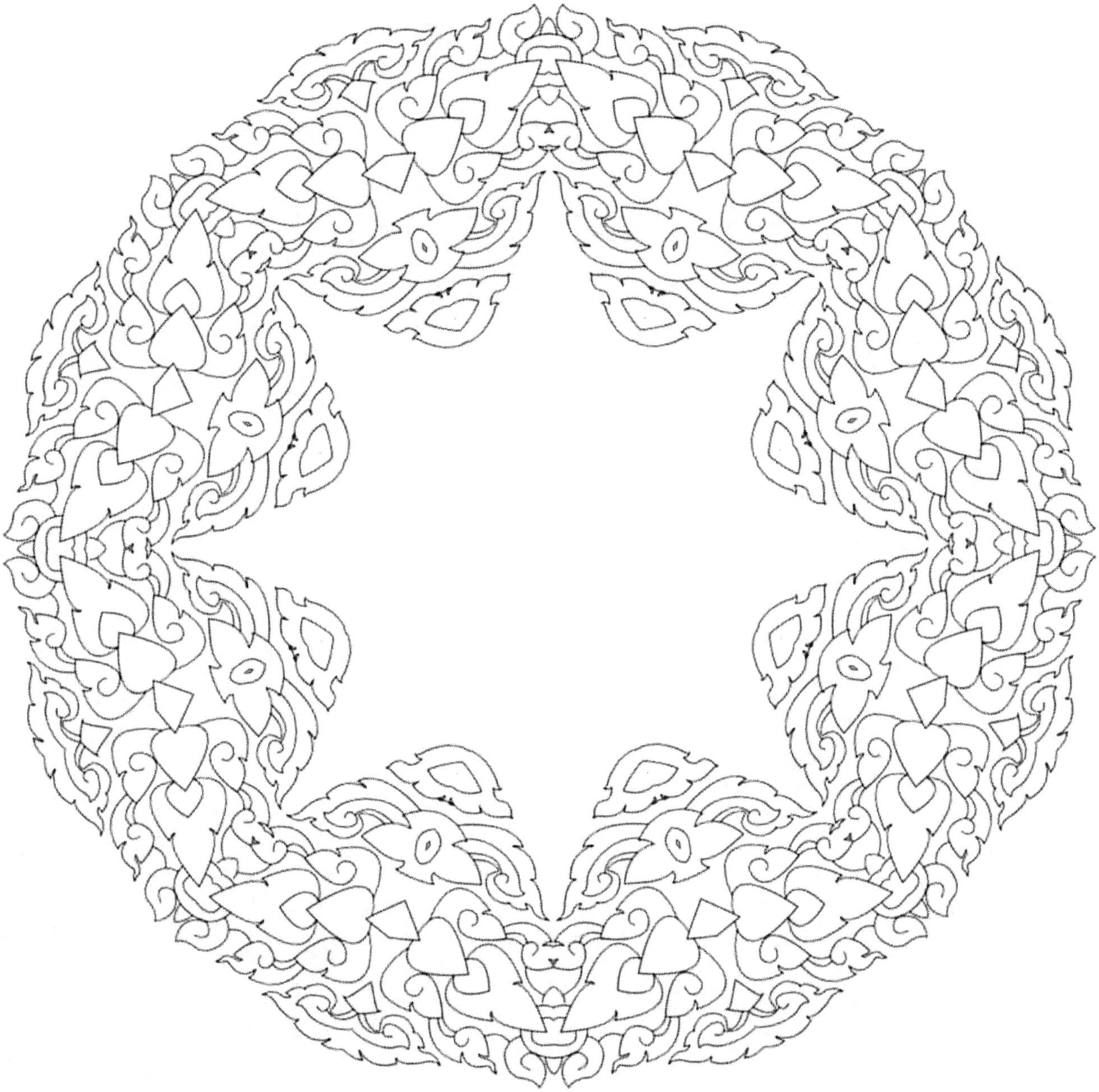

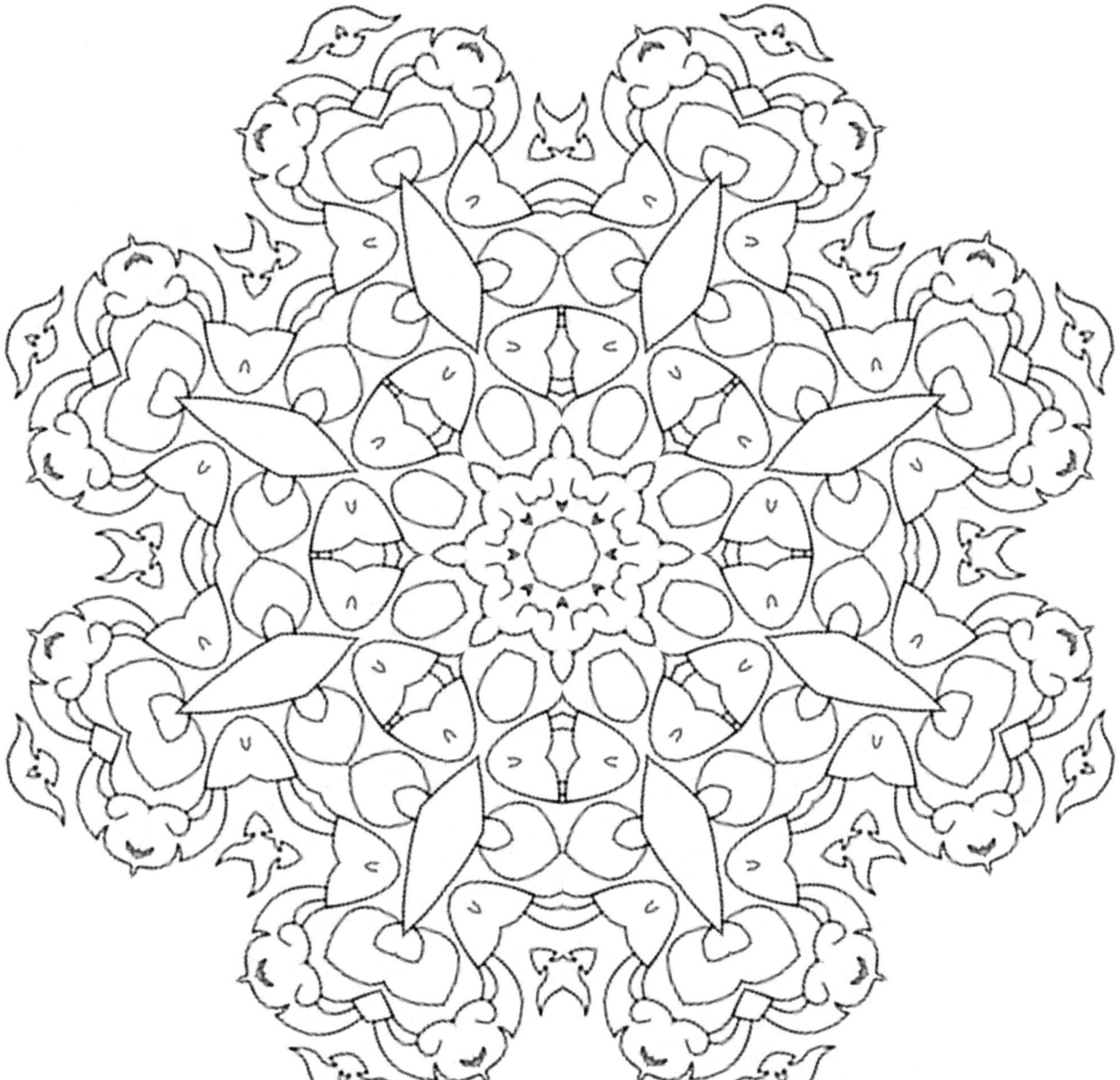

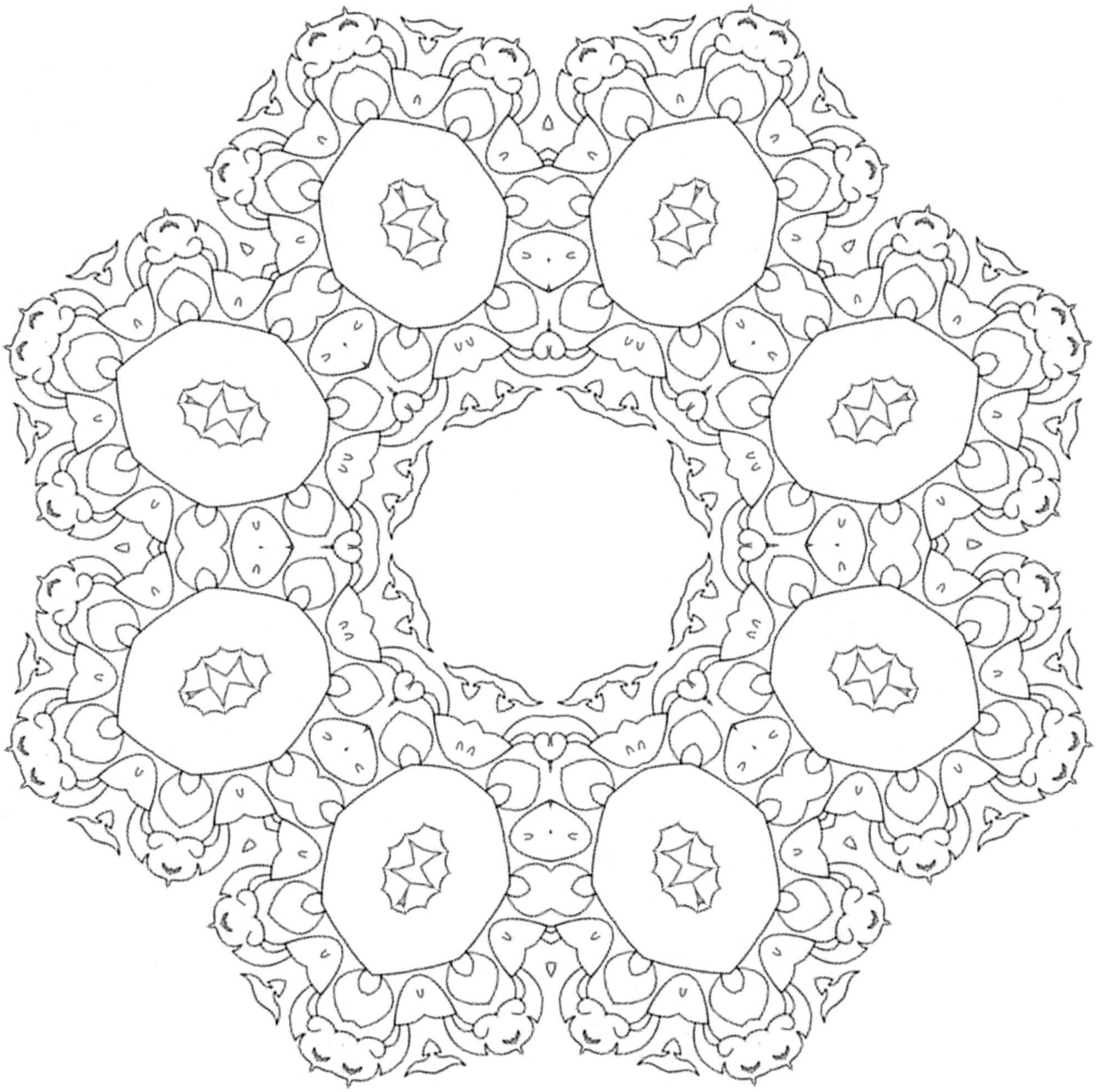

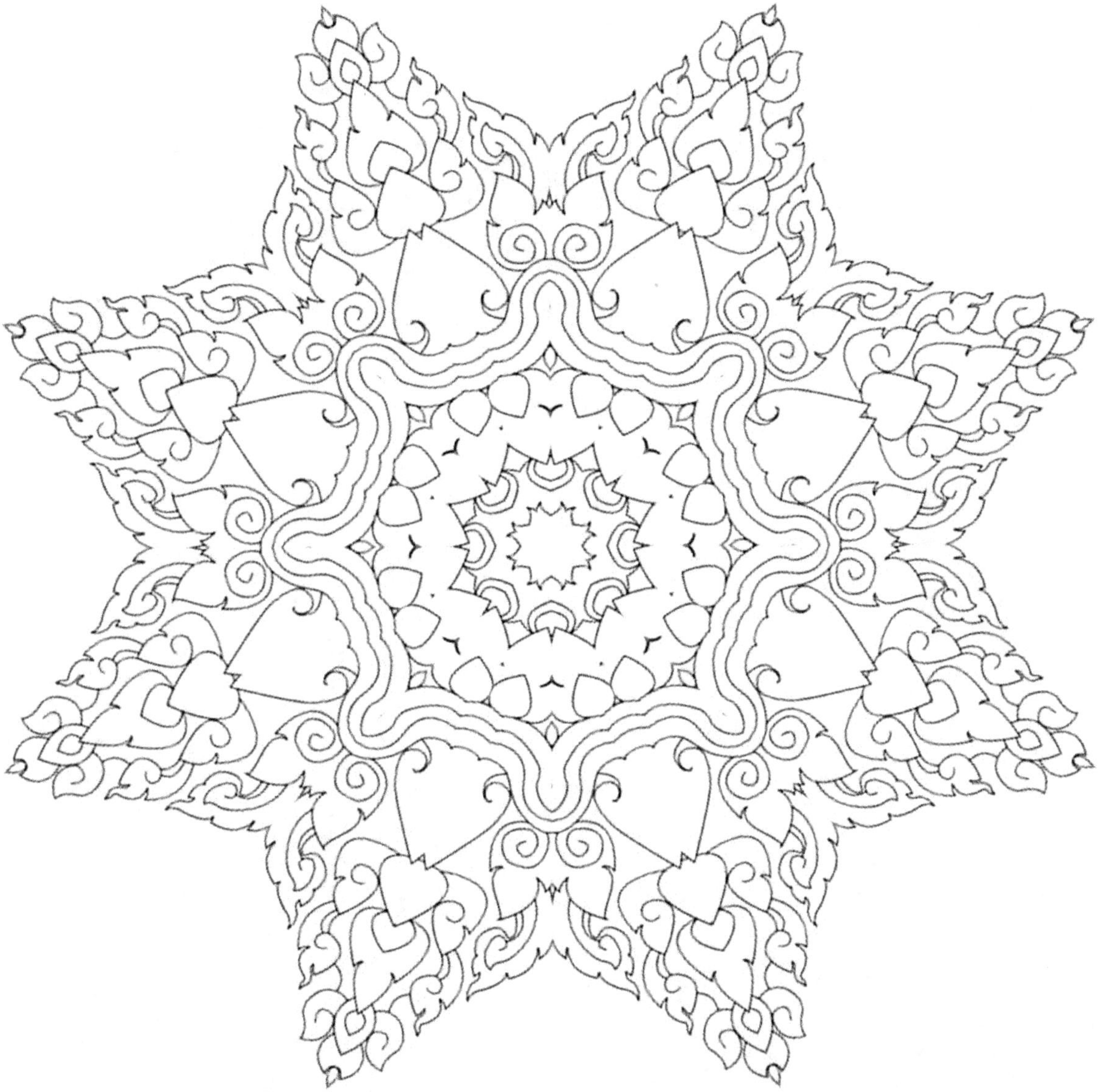

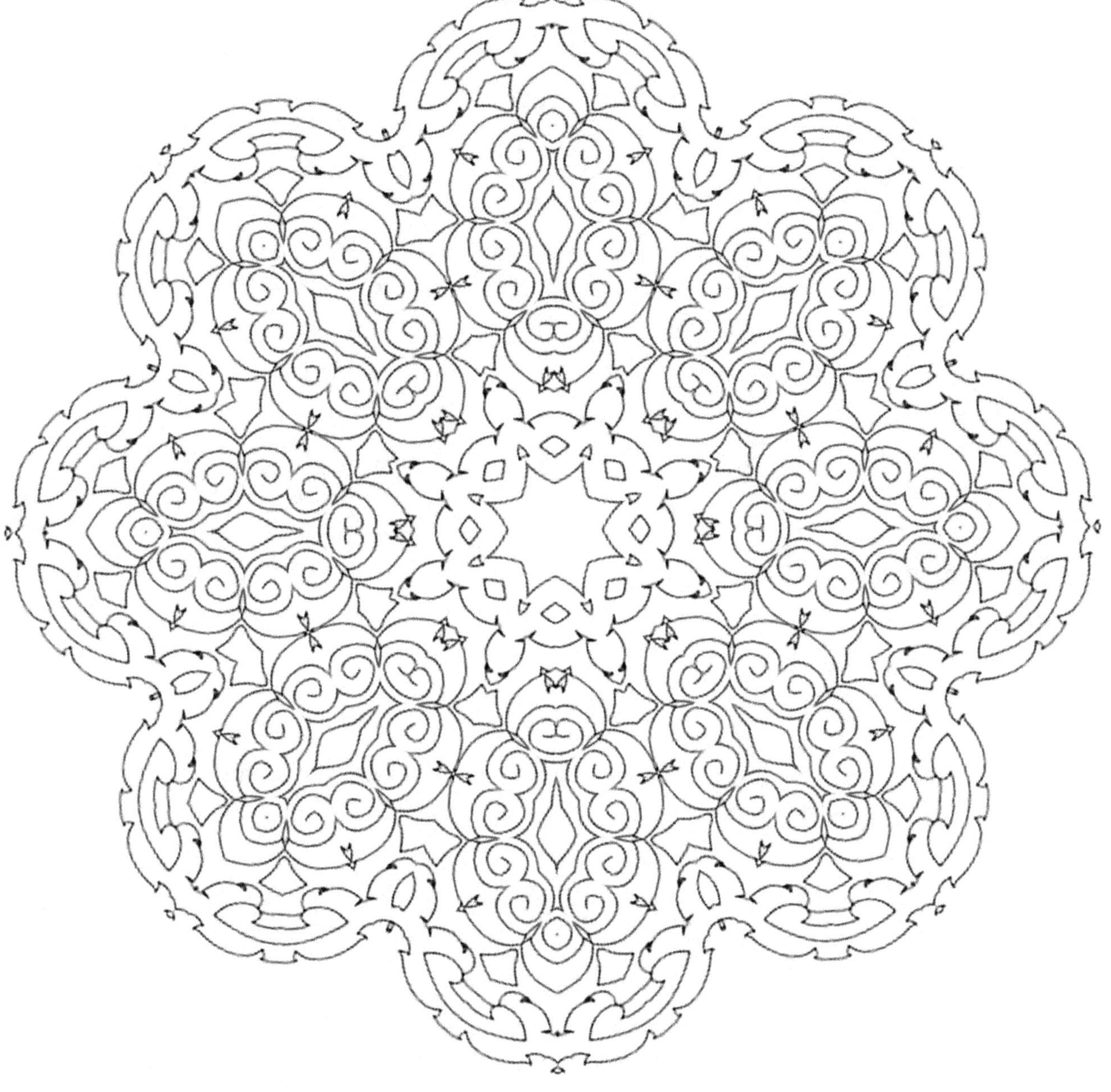

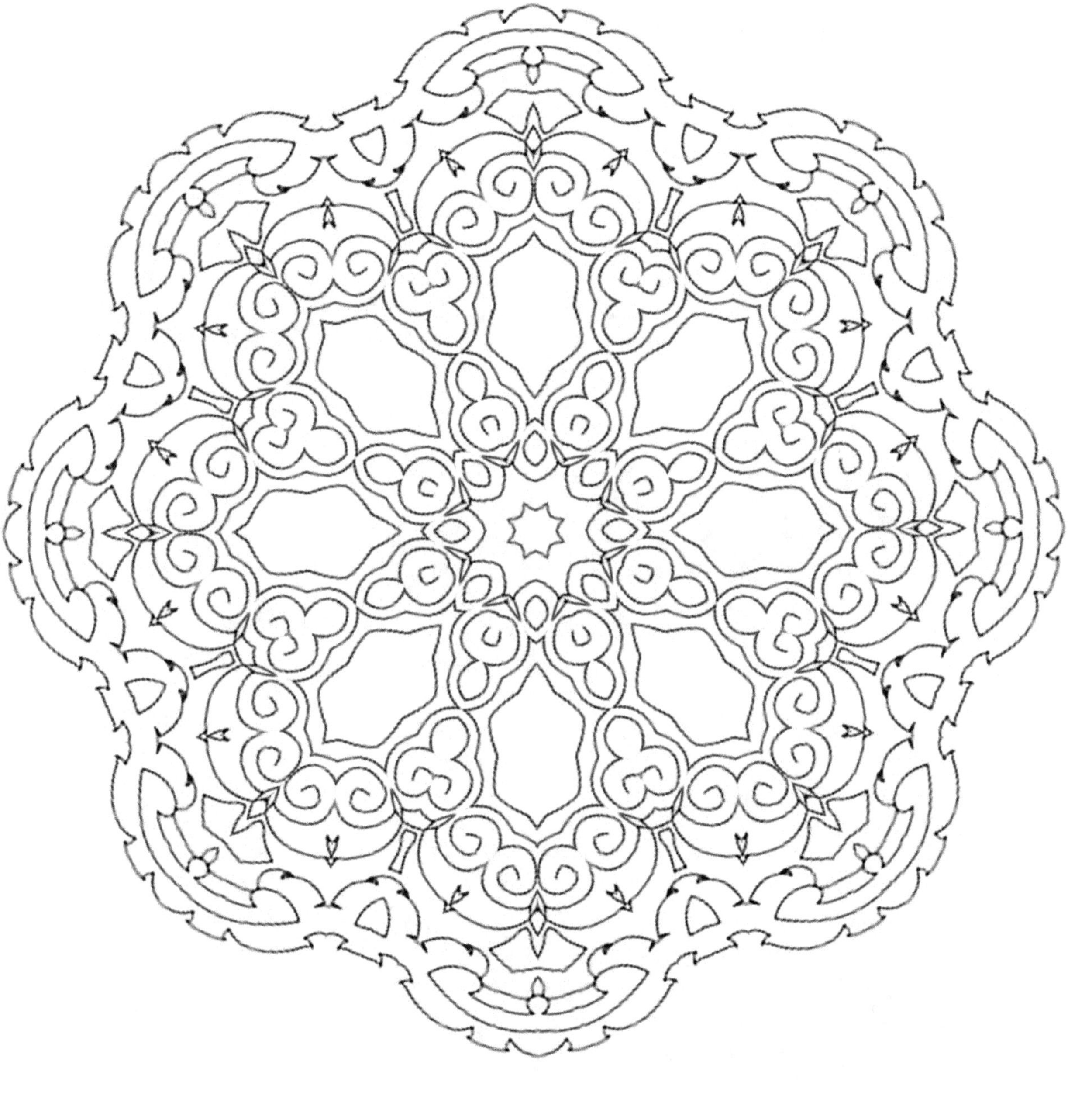

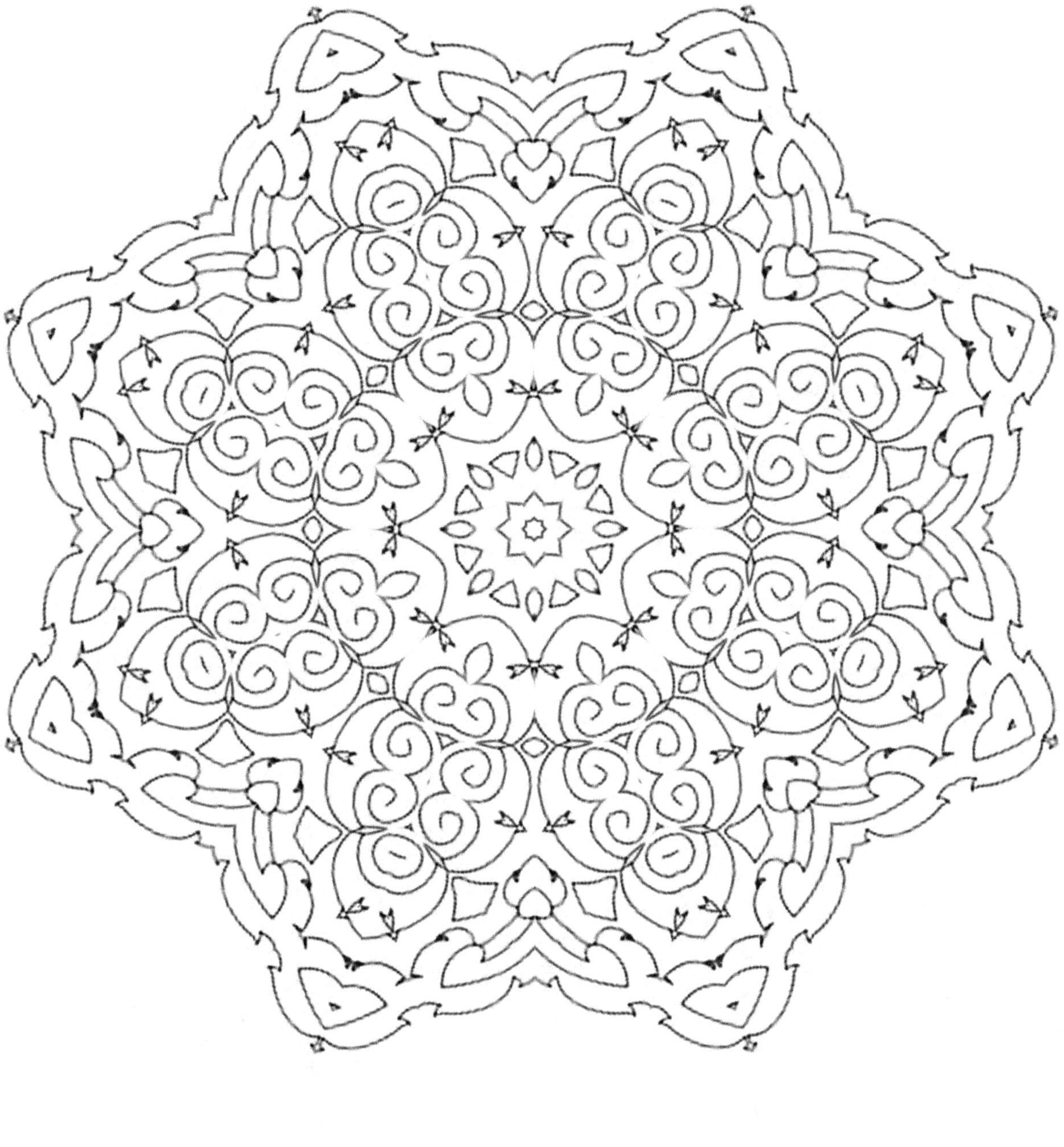

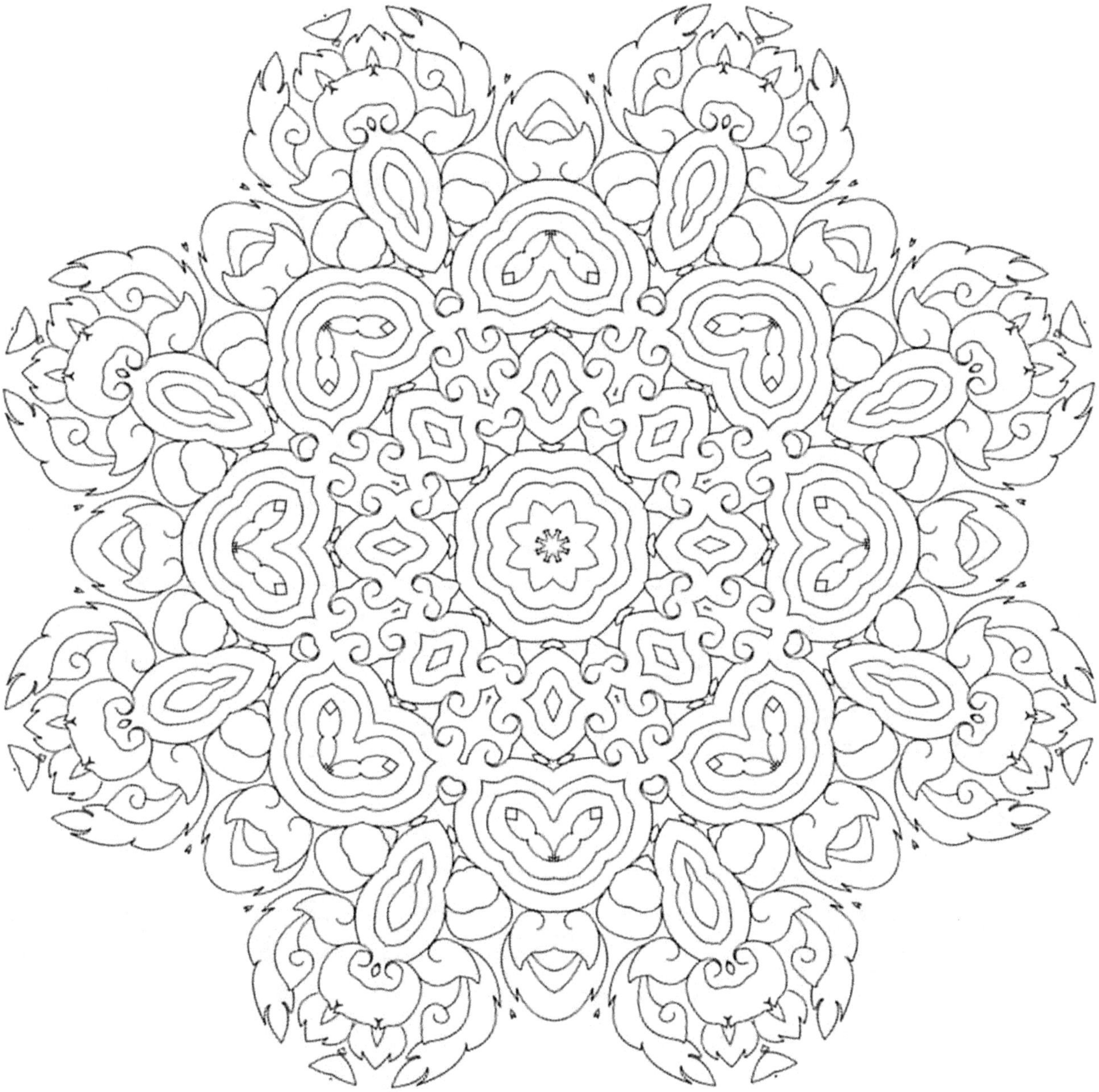

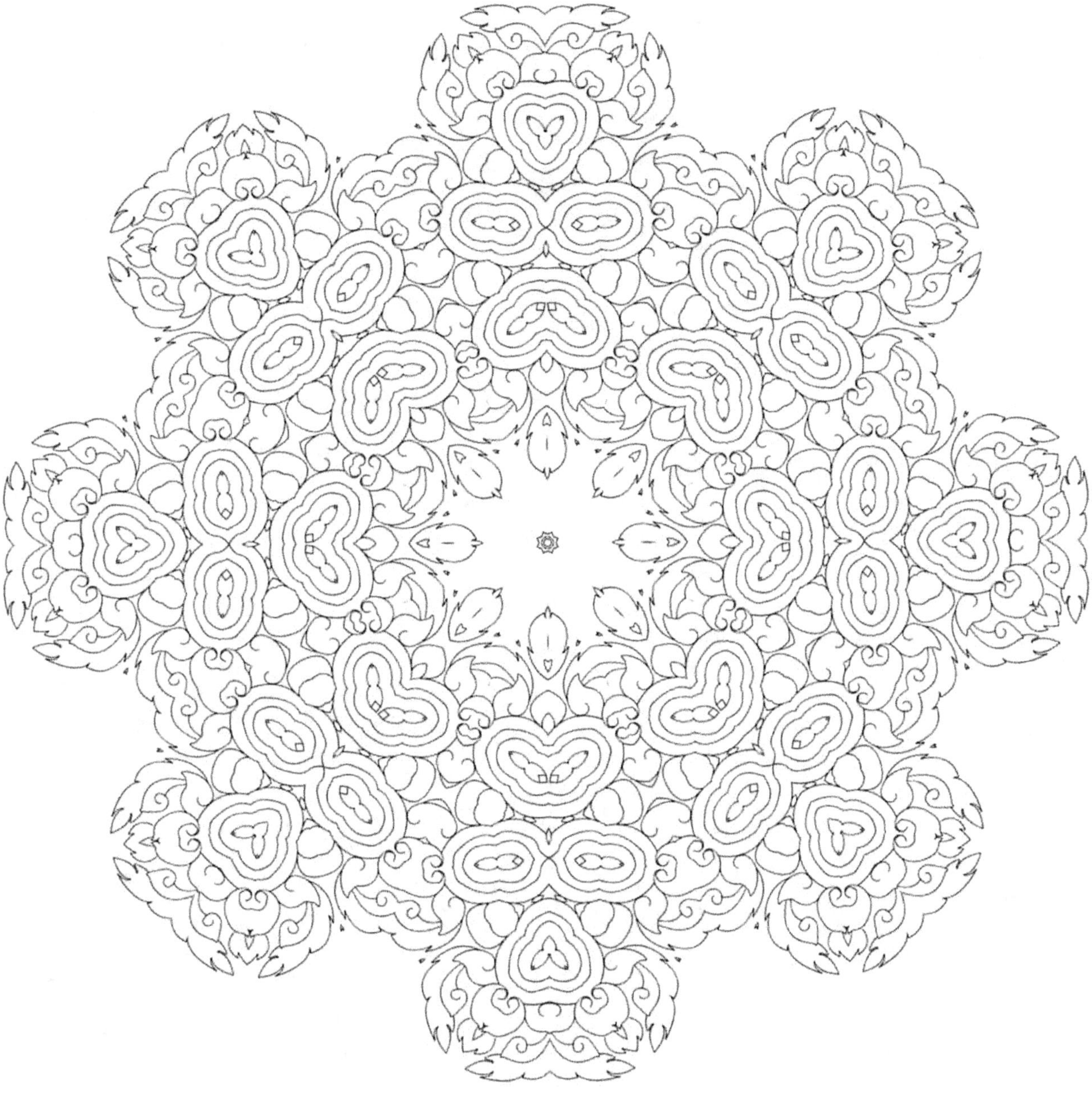

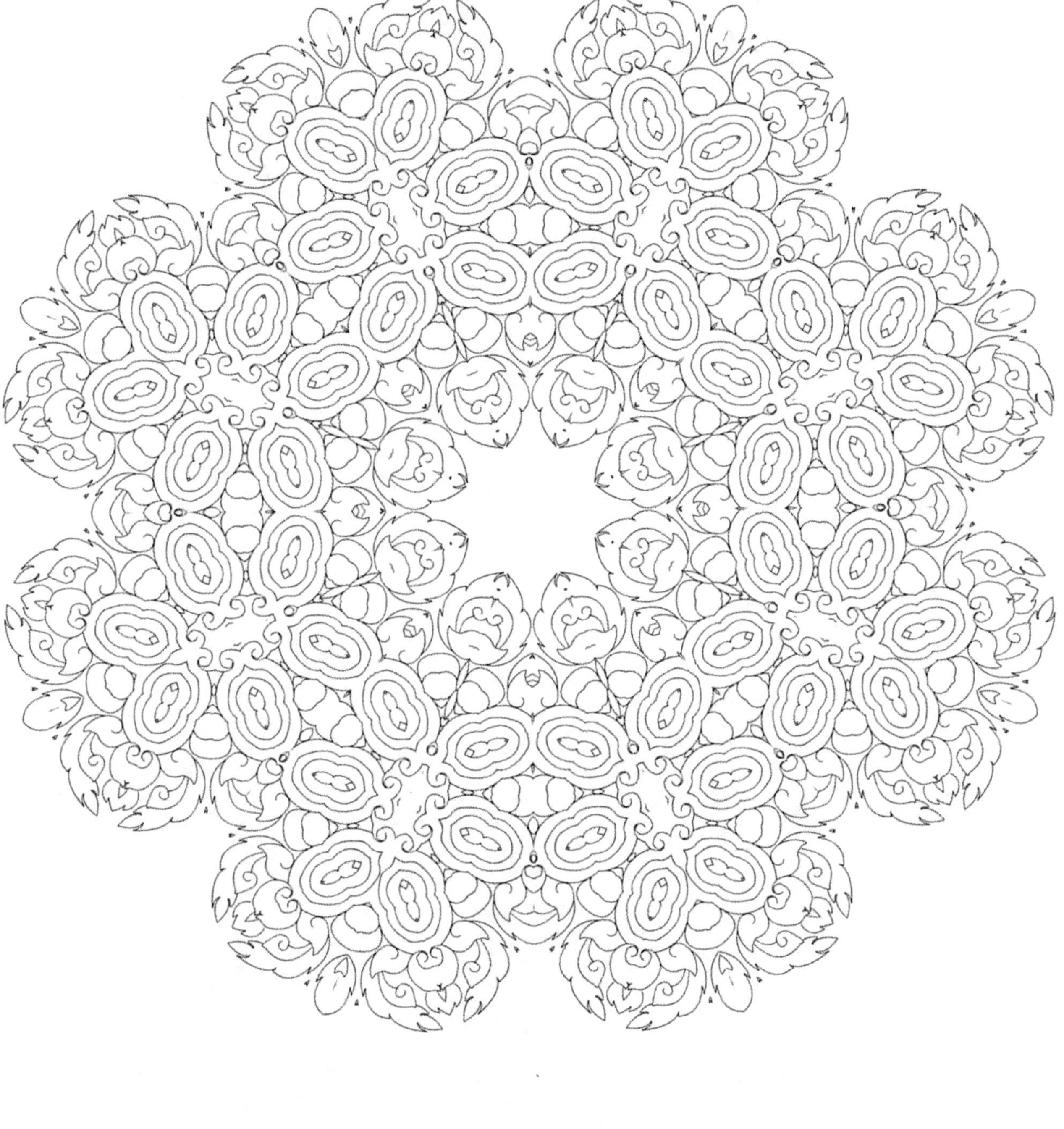

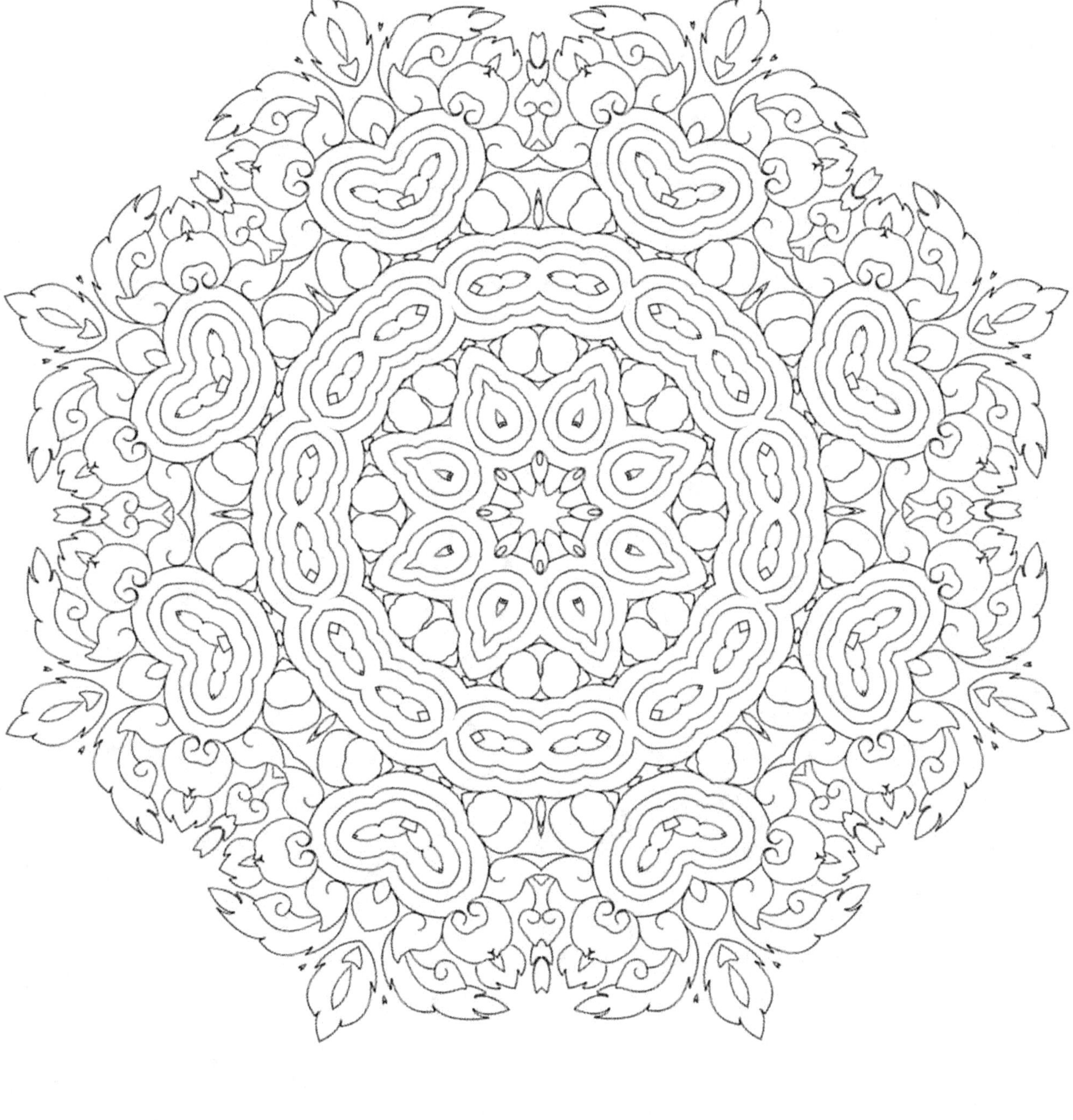

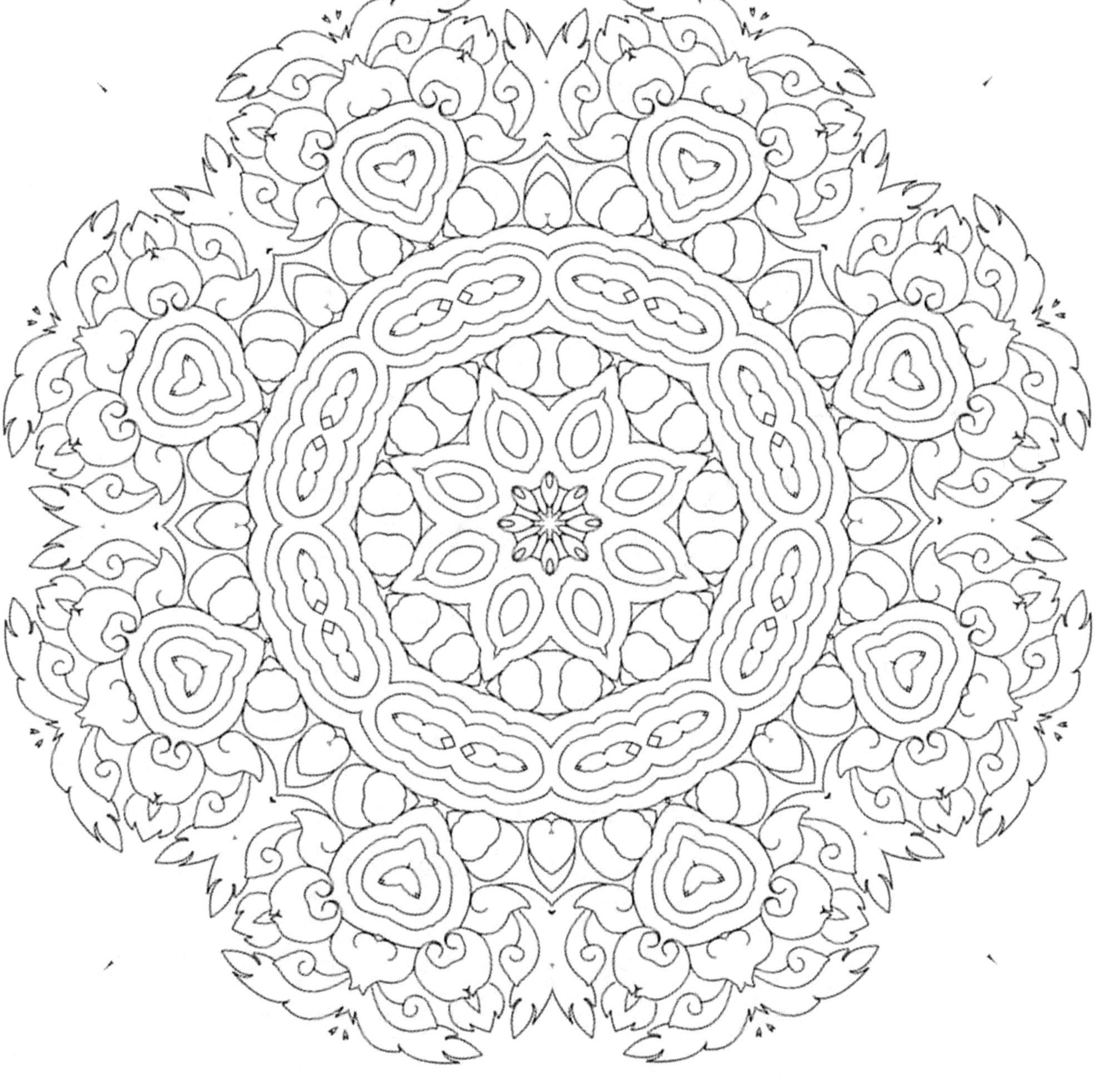

Thank you

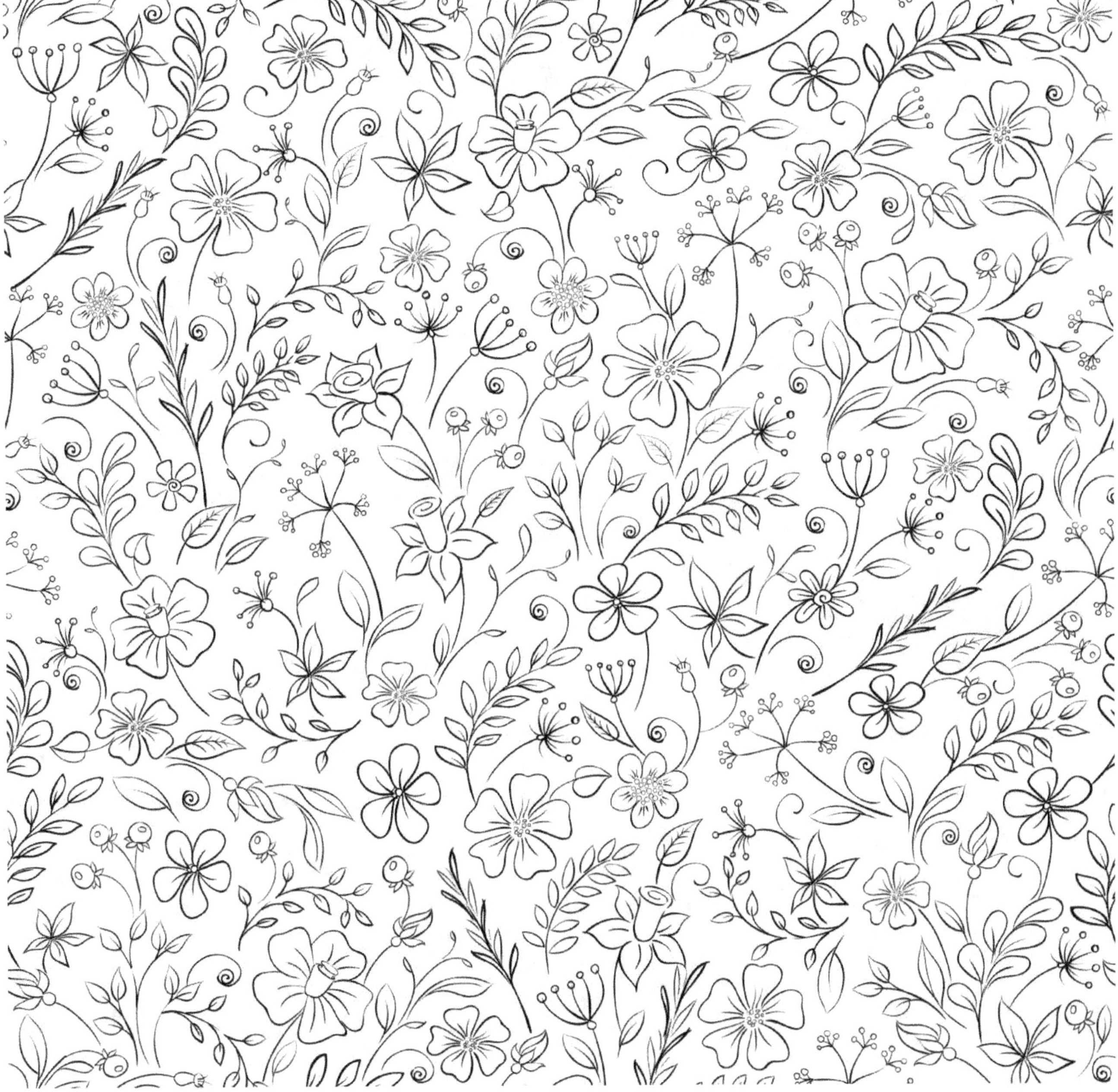

www.ingramcontent.com/pod-product-compliance
Lightning Source LLC
Chambersburg PA
CBHW081117180526
45170CB00008B/2892
9781541255340